Publicity Handbook

*for Churches
and Christian
Organizations*

COMMUNICATION IN MINISTRY

PUBLICITY HANDBOOK

for Churches and Christian Organizations

A step-by-step guide to help any Christian group get the most out of events, mailings, and publicity.

JAMES A. VITTI

Ministry Resources Library

Zondervan Publishing House • Grand Rapids, MI

PUBLICITY HANDBOOK FOR CHURCHES AND CHRISTIAN ORGANIZATIONS
Copyright © 1987 by James A. Vitti

MINISTRY RESOURCES LIBRARY is an imprint of Zondervan Publishing House, 1415 Lake Drive, S.E., Grand Rapids, Michigan 49506.

Library of Congress Cataloging in Publication Data

Vitti, James A.
   Publicity handbook for churches and Christian organizations.

   1. Church publicity—Handbooks, manuals, etc. I. Title.
BV653.V58   1987   254.4   87-13263
ISBN 0-310-37601-7

All Scripture quotations, unless otherwise noted, are taken from THE HOLY BIBLE: NEW INTERNATIONAL VERSION (North American Edition), copyright © 1973, 1978, 1984 by the International Bible Society. Used by permission of Zondervan Bible Publishers.

All rights reserved. No part of this publication may be reproduced, stored in a retrieval system, or transmitted in any form or by any means— electronic, mechanical, photocopy, recording, or any other—except for brief quotations in printed reviews or designated portions of the appendixes, without the prior permission of the publisher.

Edited by James E. Ruark
Designed by Louise Bauer

Printed in the United States of America

87 88 89 90 91 92 / CH / 10 9 8 7 6 5 4 3 2 1

This book is gratefully dedicated to those who contributed to the development of a writer:

To my parents, who wisely encouraged me to have a love for words;

To Mrs. Caryl Myers, whose dedication to teaching and to her students fueled that love for words;

To Mike Russell, whose friendship has shown me that anything can be possible;

And to Kathy, my beloved inspiration.

Contents

Preface	9
1. Let's Remember What We're All in It for	11
2. The Crucial First Step	14
3. Setting Goals: What Do We Want to Accomplish?	17
4. Strategy and Tactics: The Plan Takes Shape	25
5. Writing to Persuade	40
6. Designing to Persuade	61
7. The Mail: Our Secret Weapon	76
8. Getting It Printed and Mailed	86
9. The Follow-up	97
10. Newsletters and Brochures	100
11. Some Final Advice	106
Appendix 1. *Case Study: Seminar on Moral Development of Children*	108
Appendix 2. *Fill-in Forms: A Guide*	137
Appendix 3. *Glossary of Terms*	156

Preface

Why this book?

There are thousands of churches and Christian groups doing worthwhile things all the time. Yet a lack of time, money, and professional know-how in publicizing these projects often keeps them from fulfilling their potential.

Pastors use professional speaking techniques to communicate better in sermons. Christian writers use professional techniques to communicate better through books, magazines, brochures, and newspapers. And Christian musicians use professional techniques to communicate better through their music.

So why shouldn't Christians use professional advertising, marketing, and public relations techniques to communicate better about their happenings?

You'd never think of sending a letter on a piece of paper torn from a brown paper bag, would you? Of course not—you want to do a good job of communicating your message.

This book is a guide to going one step further—turning that good job into a *great* one. It's written for anyone who has ever volunteered—or been volunteered—to handle the publicity and wondered if there were some easier ways to do things a little better.

There are.

God has called us to be good stewards of our gifts and talents (Matt. 25:14–30). If we prayerfully use the best methods He has given us the opportunity to use—acknowledging that it is He doing the real work—we can stand before Him in peace knowing we have fulfilled our obligation well.

It is exciting to be a part of all that—and to see the results God causes to fall into place. I'd encourage you to dig in and go the extra mile, for good promotions do take more time and energy than poor promotions. But it surely is worth it!

No one knows that better than Jan Cox, without whom this book would not exist. Jan has consistently given Kevin Wahaus and me the freedom and encouragement to create fun advertising for The Church at the Crossing. Thanks, Jan.

1
Let's Remember What We're All in It for

If you're having a church getaway or a revival meeting or a Sunday school attendance drive—or *any* good, worthwhile activity, for that matter—it is all too easy to get caught up in the numbers.

"Let's get ten more men to go to Camp Hayawatha!"

"If just three more people accept Christ this weekend, we'll pass last year's figures!"

"Only $4,000 to go until we top off the bus fund."

Worthwhile goals, yes. But there's a subtle danger in losing sight of the forest for all the trees.

Let us never forget the simple reason *why* we want more people to go or join or accept or sign on the dotted line. "Whatever you do, do it all for the glory of God" (1 Cor. 10:31).

Jesus is interested in quality, not quantity. Quality of relationships—with Him and with each other.

So when we're trying to get people involved in our worthwhile activities, we really need to keep an eye on *our* part in it all. Our role may be seed-planting, or it may be watering—but God Himself is responsible for the results (1 Cor. 3:6).

The trouble is, we have a hard time recognizing the difference between *spiritual* results and *physical* results. And that's because we generally can't see the spiritual results (and if we do, it's often indirect and may take months or even years to see), while physical results can be immediate. And immediately gratifying.

One physical result we can get caught up in is body counts. We generally equate a successful event with a big turnout. That may be true in secular happenings such as a ball game or a Broadway show, but nobody's exercising spiritual gifts behind second base or revealing scriptural insight in the opening act. It is just not necessarily the case where God's church is concerned.

For instance, hundreds and even thousands may attend a given service on a given Sunday at a given church. The choir may perform magnificently in their shiny satin robes, and the pastor may deliver a foot-stomping, tear-jerking sermon that people discuss all week. But what if the church is a satanic, God-mimicking cult? The secular perspective is that the service was a great success. But in God's eyes, was this any more than a pathetic, wasteful abomination?

Sadly, the same can be true in a church that is doctrinally sound but spiritually dead. Hundreds may attend faithfully each week—but get absolutely no closer to the Lord.

Conversely, a tiny group, properly inspired and empowered by the Holy Spirit, can move mountains.

We need to consider *spiritual* results and accomplishments, not physical appearances.

So what are we to do?

God equipped us with brains and creativity and a good set of hands with which to work. So a good steward of the publicity assignment ought prayerfully to do everything possible to produce quality materials for seed-planting purposes—and then count on the Lord to produce the fruit.

Unfortunately, churches and other Christian groups have traditionally produced unprofessional materials. Microscopic budgets have been partially at fault, but now easier and cheaper access to much printing and graphic technology is helping to change all that. Additionally, Christians are beginning to use successful marketing, advertising, and public relations methods that have been known to Madison Avenue for years.

In fact, you've probably seen some of the attractive, colorful mailers and ads many Christian groups are now producing. They're producing results—both physical *and* spiritual. The main reason for their success is that they communicate the message clearly and effectively. The situation is like a farmer using modern, scientific methods instead of techniques used by his grandfather. God gives us seeds to plant, so we should use the best possible means to plant them where they belong.

If you're expecting 150 people to come to a church event and 400 show up, praise God and trust Him that He's blessing your ministry as well as those in attendance.

And if you expected 150 people to come and only 14 showed up? It's time to evaluate. Did you (and others) pray regularly and consistently, with a right motivation? Were your expectations reasonable? (In other words, did only 20 people actually hear about the event?) Were your announcements and other publicity clear, accurate, and sharply executed? Don't forget to learn from past mistakes so you won't make them again.

But also, don't forget to consider whether your goals matched the Lord's. Maybe *you* wanted 150 people to come, but maybe He wanted 14. What did the 14 get out of it? Remember: God wants quality more than quantity.

You know why you're doing what you're doing. The big task of learning to do it better lies formidably ahead. Let's have at it.

2

The Crucial First Step

When a big-time ad agency sets out to create a new campaign, the first thing the staff does is research. Followed by a marketing plan to set direction. Followed by more research.

Here is your chance to outdo the professionals, because as a Christian, with Christian goals, you won't start with research or a marketing plan. You'll start with prayer.

Note a subtle distinction here: prayer is *not* the *first step* in a marketing plan. In fact, it's not even a part of the marketing plan. Prayer precedes and completely overshadows the marketing plan.

That's pretty important, really. If prayer were simply a *part* of the marketing plan, it could potentially be equated with writing copy and mailing brochures. It could also potentially put the focus on us and our works instead of glorifying God by trusting Him to get the results He wants.

The Lord's job is to get the results; it's our job to do the executing and handle the paperwork. Professional advertising, marketing, and public relations techniques are simply *tools* by which we can be good stewards—nothing more. God's supernatural intervention in answer to prayer is the method by which new members will come or funds will be raised.

Here are some important things to keep in mind when praying about the aspect of ministry you'll be promoting:

1. HAVE A RIGHT ATTITUDE

First, make sure your heart's in the right place. That means you personally must have a solid, day-by-day walk with the Lord as well as a right attitude about the specific task ahead.

In John 15:7 Jesus promised that if we're abiding in Him, we'll receive what we request in prayer. That's an interesting verse in that there are two ways to look at it.

It means that as we're abiding in Him, we'll be sensitive to the Holy Spirit's will—and thus be praying about things the Spirit desires. So it makes sense we'll see our prayers answered, since we're asking for things God wants us to ask for in the first place.

Does the verse also mean that if we're walking with Jesus, our prayers will be answered—whereas if we're not, our prayers will go unanswered?

Several times in the Old Testament, God calls the prayers and sacrifices of the wicked abominable. Proverbs 15:29 even goes as far as to say the Lord is far away from wicked people, but hears the prayers of the righteous.

So before we begin to pray about the future positive results of our event, we must make sure we and others are praying for each person's relationship with Jesus.

We should also remember that He wants us to come boldly into His presence (Hebrews 4:16), to claim His victories in advance with confidence (1 John 5:14), and to ask and receive—so *we* may be joyful in Him (John 16:24). Armed with those attitudes, we should have clear channels of communication open with our Lord.

2. PRAY SPECIFICALLY

The Lord wants us to be specific in our prayers. So pray for things like the weather the day of the event, open hearts and minds in the editors you'll be contacting, and even specific people you'd like to have attend.

Matthew 6 offers some good guidelines about specific prayer, including an admonition against vague, general repetitions. Tell God exactly what you want to happen. The more specific our prayers, the more opportunity there will be for specific *answers*.

3. YOU'D BETTER BELIEVE IT

It never fails. Even though we see a tremendous answer to prayer, we turn right around and don't trust God for something else. We're all just a little bit too much like the Israelites who had to wander in the wilderness for forty years because of their lack of faith. But we can trust God will do *great* things. James 5:15–16 tells us to ask with faith; Matthew 7:7 promises that prayers will be answered, and Matthew 21:22 promises that whatever we ask—as long as we believe—will be done.

Better still, God often answers prayer differently and in much better ways than we expect (Eph. 3:20–21). Let's leave the door open for those kinds of miracles to happen.

4. PRAY, PRAY, PRAY, AND PRAY AGAIN

Finally, we have to *keep on praying*. With others (Matt. 18:19) and alone with the Lord (Matt. 6:6). Not just a one-time quickie, but regular prayer before, during, and after the promotion and event. Paul understood this principle, as exemplified by his telling the Thessalonians to pray *without ceasing* (1 Thess. 5:17).

Be sure to enlist others for prayer support, too.

Having taken this first step, it's time to use the communication skills and tools God has given us.

3

Setting Goals: What Do We Want to Accomplish?

The first step toward successful communication is goal-setting. Before we can achieve anything, we have to decide what we want to accomplish. And it's always a good idea to put it in writing. Writing down our goals can help us define them—and achieve them.

A key part of this purpose, our *objective* statement, should be simple and precise—so simple that it can be stated in one sentence. Here are some examples:

> Persuade men, ages 29–54, with at least two children, to purchase a Ford Econoline van.
>
> Persuade men and women to choose AT&T as their long-distance carrier.
>
> Persuade North Central High School students to attend Friday's "Teen Life" meeting.

Notice a few similarities in these examples:

1. All begin with the word "persuade." That's what we want to do—persuade someone why he or she should *do*

something, whether it's buying a van, selecting a phone company, or coming to our event.

No one is going to do what we want them to do unless we can persuade them they should. The next few chapters will examine just *how* to persuade them; at this point we're just deciding what it is we want them to think, feel, or do.

2. Notice the attention given to *whom* we're trying to persuade. Marketing people call this a *target audience.*

If we're trying to raise funds to add a new wing to the church building, our primary target audience will be the people who attend our church. A secondary target audience might include former members who have moved and other Christians who live in the vicinity. A tertiary target audience might include interested members of the community.

How do we identify the target audience? Generally it's pretty clear because the target audience has already been "selected" for us. For example, for most church activities and projects, it's the people who attend the church. If you're a campus minister, it's the people on the campus. If you're a missionary in Oconomowoc, the target audience is the population of Oconomowoc.

Depending on who makes up our target audience base, there are generally different ways to reach different groups.

> If we're advertising golf clubs, we probably would have commercials on televised golf tournaments.
>
> If we're marketing computer software for oil rig operators, we'd probably run ads in oil industry trade publications.
>
> On the other hand, we wouldn't run a beer ad in *Christianity Today* or a nail polish ad in *Sports Illustrated*. The target audience doesn't match up with the readership of those publications.
>
> Yet if we're having a church picnic and the church happens to be in Los Angeles, we

SETTING GOALS: WHAT DO WE WANT TO ACCOMPLISH?

wouldn't necessarily run an ad in the *Los Angeles Times*. We may end up reaching most of our target audience, but we'll also reach very many people who *aren't* in our target audience.

Marketers call the people we reach but don't need to reach "waste" (for obvious reasons). The trouble is, we pay for every person who sees our ad, so we want as little waste circulation as possible. That is partially why we need to define our target audience quite specifically at the outset.

3. Notice that our objectives statement must end with a specific, detailed action: Buy a van. Choose AT&T. Come to the meeting.

What do we want people to do? Increase their tithe? Attend the elder's meeting? Bake a cake for the bazaar? Say it. Just that simply. Got the idea? Let's try a few more.

> Persuade members of Faith Church to attend the Sunday Night Film Festival.
>
> Persuade homeowners with property adjoining the First Baptist Church parking lot to sign the zoning petition.
>
> Persuade residents of Rancho Cordova to bring their cars to the all-church car wash.

In some cases we may have more than one objective for a single event:

> Persuade members to make a one-time gift and increase their weekly tithe to at least 10 percent.

THE MARKETING PLAN

Now that we've written a first-class objective statement, we're well on our way into the marketing plan.

The marketing plan is a one-or-two-page list of summary statements about what we want to accomplish. This is an essential first step toward any successful promotional activity. The marketing plan has two main functions:

1. It helps us to see, clarify, and refine the project. As we're putting down on paper and/or discussing ideas about the plan, it will help us discover the direction to take.

2. It acts as a road map to keep us on track once we've started. Everything that follows should be matched up against the marketing plan to see if it is working to achieve the goals we've set at the beginning.
Often someone may have an idea that sounds great after we've started, but that, when examined in light of the marketing plan, may not be appropriate for achieving our goals. So it protects us from getting off course.

There are several ways to organize a marketing plan, but they usually have some basic things in common. This is a typical sequence:

> Historical information
> Objectives
> Strategy
> Tactics
> Evaluation
> Budget

Now let's take a closer look at each component.

HISTORICAL INFORMATION

Historical information is simply what's happened when we've done this type of event before. For instance:

> Last year, we used direct mail, public service announcements on radio and TV, bulletin inserts, and briefs in newspaper church columns. A total of 210 people attended the seminar; 180 of these responded to the mailing of 1,500; 25 came in

response to the bulletin insert; and 5 came from other sources. The cost was $185; the gross income was $2,100.

There are some pretty important pearls of insight there, wouldn't you say? We can assume mail worked well, for example, so we'd probably want to try it again.

As with the objectives statement, keep the historical brief. Just list the ways you publicized the event and how well each worked. Unfortunately, there may be little or no historical information. That's all right, but try to make it a point of generating some this time—so the job will be a lot easier next time. Or, as they say, so we don't have to spend a lot of time reinventing the wheel!

OBJECTIVES

Guess what! This part's already done. Just plug in the objectives statement that's already developed:

Persuade women who attend the North Avenue Church to come to the Ladies Night Banquet.

STRATEGY

Strategy involves which media we'll use (such as mail, radio, newspapers, and bulletin inserts) as well as the creative approach we'll take. The next chapter will explain how to develop the strategy.

TACTICS

Tactics are specific applications of a strategy. In other words, if our *strategy* says to use local TV, a *tactic* would be to use channels 5 and 29. The next chapter will also explain how to make strategy and tactics work together.

EVALUATION

Our marketing plan should explain how we intend to evaluate how well we reached our objectives. If our objective was

Persuade 100 members to attend the potluck.

the evaluation statement should read something like

Compare actual attendance figures with objectives.

Other objectives/evaluation statements include

> OBJECTIVE: Persuade church members to donate $5,000 to the bus fund.
>
> EVALUATION: Compare dollar amount given with objective.
>
> OBJECTIVE: Persuade members to return choir evaluation forms with constructive comments.
>
> EVALUATION: Was ample feedback received?

And don't forget to actually *apply* and examine the evaluation after everything's finished ... because that becomes next year's "historical"!

BUDGET

If you have a set amount to work with, this task is simple:

Budget is $250.

Or, more commonly,

There is no budget.

Generally, if there's "no money," but you can use the church copier and stamps, determine the limit on the number of copies.

SETTING GOALS: WHAT DO WE WANT TO ACCOMPLISH?

There is no budget allocated, but we can make 100 copies and send them with 100 letters.

Don't be discouraged if most of the budget statements sound like that; we can do *great* things on a shoestring. Even postcards can be tremendously successful, for instance.

Remember, *what* we say is a lot more important than *how* we say it. As long as we're getting the message out, most of the battle is already won. And there are some creative techniques in later chapters in this book that work just fine straight off the copy machine.

THE WHOLE PLAN

Not *too* tough, is it? Here's an entire marketing plan:

BAKE SALE MARKETING PLAN

HISTORICAL INFORMATION: Last year we relied on word-of-mouth and the bulletin. We made $45.71 for the missions fund at no cost.

OBJECTIVES: Persuade members of the church and community within a five-mile radius of the church to come to our bake sale and buy something.

STRATEGY: Announcements at church and in the bulletin.
Mailing to members.
Posters and handbills.
Public service announcements on radio and TV.
Press releases to newspapers.

TACTICS: Announcements in church services and in the bulletin February 5, 12, 19, and 26.
Mailing to 297 members February 27.

PUBLICITY HANDBOOK FOR CHURCHES

100 posters, distributed by Charlie, Bessie, and Curly at local shops; 100 handbills distributed by Fred, Ethel, Peewee, and Lucy at the 4-Corners Mall Saturday morning, March 4.

:10 and :30 PSAs to WXYZ, WQQQ, WXAZ radio and channels 7, 9, and 21; follow-up phone call.

Press release to the *Indianapolis Star* religion editor and to the "Washington Township Weekly Topics" editor; follow-up phone call.

EVALUATION: Compare amount spent vs. amount made; evaluate in light of last year's sales.

BUDGET: $50 for printing, plus office funds for copying and mailing.

There you have it—a real live marketing plan for your church event. Just as the big boys have on Madison Avenue.

You can do it. Start off by filling in the blanks, if necessary, with the unique features of your activity, and you'll be pretty close to the mark.

Congratulations! Now you're ready to be a creative genius.

4

Strategy and Tactics: The Plan Takes Shape

It's a Sunday afternoon in January. There is a crisp chill in the air, but inside the den a warm fire glows beside the television set. A commercial break interrupts Super Bowl XXIII.

"Hey, Erma, come look at this!"

Erma hurries in, and Max points to the set.

". . . that's right," the announcer continues, "the Second Avenue Church of Greenwood will be having its annual Winter Banquet this Thursday night at seven o'clock sharp—we're looking forward to seeing you there. And God bless!"

Unlikely? Very. Thirty-second commercial time during major specials like the Super Bowl and some prime-time programs costs several hundred thousand dollars. The commercials themselves sometimes cost almost that much to produce. So what options does a humble church have to publicize its events?

Plenty. In this chapter we take a closer look at most of them and see how they fit into our strategy.

MEDIA

The strategy section of our marketing plan is primarily a media selection process. When we select which media to use, we'll evaluate in light of the strengths and weaknesses of each specific medium.

The media we're most likely to consider include

> Announcements at church
> Church bulletin
> Church newsletter
> Direct mail
> Posters
> Magazines
> Newspapers
> Radio
> Television
> Handouts/flyers

Realistically, we should be able to use almost all these media at virtually no cost—if we know how. So don't worry about not being able to get the word out; there are no less than *ten* options on this list! (And it doesn't even include skywriting!)

ANNOUNCEMENTS AT CHURCH

This one's pretty easy. The key point to remember is to plan early as to which days to make the announcement and to see that the pastor (or whoever is in charge of announcements) is well informed as to our plans. Since this one is free and very direct to our target audience, it should *always* be included in our strategy for a church event.

CHURCH BULLETIN

Again, this is pretty much a matter of planning ahead. If we can go as far as having the event publicized on a separate bulletin insert, great! Chapters 5 and 6 will provide some tips on preparing a successful insert. This is another medium that should *always* be included in our strategy.

CHURCH NEWSLETTER

If our church or group has a newsletter, this also is an ideal medium to use. (If there is no newsletter, serious consideration should be given to starting one.) Talk to the editor to see how prominently the event can be displayed or, if you just happen to be the editor, play it up as you see fit.

Be aware of deadlines. Don't expect to get an article accepted for the newsletter on September 29 if the publication is supposed to be in the mail October 1—it's probably too late. Newsletters are planned in advance, so be sure you know when material is due for the appropriate issue.

DIRECT MAIL

One of the most successful admen in the world calls direct mail his "great love and secret weapon." It can be ours, too.

If used properly, direct mail can be a dramatically effective tool in publicizing our event. It's so important to Christian promotion, in fact, that chapter 7 is devoted entirely to this medium.

Direct mail is simply a mailing to the target audience, whether it's a letter, a brochure, or even a package.

When doing a mailing, we have a distinctive edge over the big, national direct mail companies. Many people are resistant to "junk mail," but most of our target audience won't perceive a letter from church as junk mail. We're encountering an audience which, as a whole, is glad to be getting some information from church.

If the budget allows, we should include direct mail in our campaign. It works. And it will continue to work.

POSTERS

In advertising jargon, posters are referred to as "outdoor" advertising. But we're not calling it that here, because we're likely to use posters indoors more than outdoors.

If we're in a big city, the cost of billboard advertising is prohibitive—up to thousands of dollars a month in some places. Even signs on buses or cabs can be extremely expensive.

But that doesn't stop us from doing little posters. Primarily we can post these on bulletin boards around the church or, if we're on a campus, around school. Some communities have places where people can put up posters, and a few friendly store owners may let us put a poster in their window—if we ask first!

You can have colorful posters printed or hand-painted, but it's very likely that we will settle for running them off on the church copier on 8½" x 11" paper. So while that probably limits us to using just black ink, at least we'll be able to use different colored paper. And, if there aren't too many posters, maybe we can find someone who'll be willing to use some felt pens to color in a few spots to help grab people's attention.

Like direct mail, posters are virtually indispensable in our strategy—even if it only means putting one in the church lobby.

If there is a huge budget, we may want to call an outdoor advertising company and inquire about billboard rates in the area. Look under "Advertising—Outdoor" in the Yellow Pages. In a large city, the listing may not be in the consumer Yellow Pages, but only in the business-to-business Yellow Pages. The local library should have such a directory, or one can be obtained from the telephone company business office.

MAGAZINES

After considering announcements, the bulletin, the newsletter, mail, and posters, our attention turns to mass

STRATEGY AND TACTICS: THE PLAN TAKES SHAPE

media: magazines, newspapers, TV, and radio. Which makes things a little more interesting.

There are two ways to approach most mass media. One is for free space. The other is paid advertising.

To oversimplify a point, free space is generally called "public relations," while space you pay for is called "advertising." In most cases, the better course is probably public relations.

Most good-sized cities now have "city magazines," and some bigger cities have more than one (the capital of Indiana, for instance, has *Indianapolis Magazine, Indianapolis Monthly,* and *Indianapolis Woman*). If you're in or near a large metropolitan area, a city magazine is a possibility.

Try to find a copy of a recent issue. See if it includes a calendar section or something similar where your event may get a listing. If there is such a section, send a press release to the section editor and follow up a few days later with a phone call.

A press release is simply a fancy name for an announcement of what's happening. There is a right way to prepare one that will increase the likelihood that it'll be printed, and there's a wrong way to do it—which is why most press releases end up in a wastebasket somewhere. Chapters 5 and 6 offer a basic outline on how to present a press release the right way.

Regarding the "section editor": We look through the first few pages of our copy of the magazine until we see a box filled with tiny type, usually near the table of contents. Somewhere in there we will probably find a listing for something like "Calendar Editor" or "Focus Editor," or whatever the magazine calls its events section. So if it says, "Calendar Editor, Fran Klepnick," we should mail the press release to

> Fran Klepnick
> Calendar Editor
> Duluth Monthly
> P. O. Box 975
> Duluth, MN 55800

If there doesn't seem to be an appropriate name or address, just call the magazine and ask the receptionist to whom the material should be sent.

Which poses a problem. Fran is a woman, right? Be careful with names. Editors are people, too, and if we call Fran a "Ms." and Fran happens to be a weightlifter with a handlebar mustache, we may have just diluted our chances of getting a press release in next month's issue.

Which poses yet another problem. If we're having a cookout on October 12, and the October issue comes out October 1, when should we send in our press release? Surely September 1 ought to be early enough.

No.

Okay, then August 1 will be early enough. Undoubtedly.

Undoubtedly not.

Magazines work so far in advance that it boggles the minds of those not in the magazine business. Generally, two to three months ahead is about right.

The trouble is, our event may not be scheduled that far ahead. In that case, magazines may not fit into our strategy.

Here's how to find out:

First, make a list of all the magazines in the area that apply. There should be a listing under "Magazines" or "Publishers—Periodical" in the Yellow Pages. Remembering our target audience, we may want to scratch a few off the list right away. For example, I'd probably eliminate *Indiana Beverage Life*, *Medical Information Systems*, and *Wholesale Drugs* immediately. We must use common sense based on our message and our target audience.

Once we have a good list, we can get on the phone and ask about their closing dates for the calendar. We should keep a record of this so we won't have to make all these calls again next time.

If we're really ahead of things—say, four or five months— we might ask the receptionist for the name of the person responsible for story ideas. If we really think our event is unique or unusual or will involve a tremendous number of people (perhaps several hundred), we should call that person and tell him or her what is planned. Once in a while it may be deemed worthy of a feature and a reporter may be sent to write a little article on the event.

Just remember two points here. First, we get caught up in what we're doing, but not everybody else will. We should try to be as objective as possible; and we should approach an editor only if we *really* have something special that can relate to the magazine's audience. If we go to an editor more than once or twice with something he or she doesn't consider worthwhile, we'll probably destroy our chances for when something special *does* come up. Remember the little boy who cried wolf.

Second, an article *before* the event is *much* better than one describing the event after it's all over. Prior coverage will generate interest, one hopes, and spur more involvement; post-event coverage, while pleasing, is probably going to be limited to being little more than an ego-gratifier. If we have a really terrific writer friend who has the time to help, he or she might be willing to write a feature story on the event and submit it to a magazine. Most magazines accept freelance work, and in fact most "city" magazines rely almost solely on freelance articles. They generally will pay a small amount, too, perhaps $50 to $100 or more.

If we are sending a feature, we will call the appropriate editor first to get some hints on what he or she is looking for. A few days after sending the article, we will call again as a follow-up. That follow-up call, incidentally, is often the difference between being published and not being published.

Ads in magazines generally cost a few hundred dollars for small, black-and-white ads to several thousand dollars for a color page—even in local publications.

Even if the budget allows for spending that kind of money, however, be careful. This is where our objectives come in. Does the magazine's readership match our target audience? Will there be a great deal of waste? Is our event of such universal appeal and interest that the magazine is a worthwhile medium to use?

If we decide that it is, we can call the magazine and ask for a media kit. They'll mail us a kit of information for advertisers which will provide information such as costs, size requirements, and facts about their "typical" reader. Also, the magazine's advertising manager would be glad to talk about whether the magazine would be suitable for our purposes.

As a general rule, magazine *ads* aren't appropriate for church events because of cost, target audience considerations, and lead time.

Yet if the timetable *isn't* a problem in our situation, we should consider trying *press releases* in local magazines.

NEWSPAPERS

As with magazines, newspapers can provide free space as well as ad space.

In most areas, there is a daily newspaper (or perhaps two) that many people read as well as a few local weekly papers. We will probably be amazed at how many newspapers in our area are listed in the Yellow Pages.

Again, eliminate a few that aren't appropriate based on target audience. For instance, if we're in East St. Louis and there's a listing for a weekly paper on the west side of town twenty-five miles away, we'd be better off saving our time and postage. And newspapers like *The Auto Trader* or *Real Estate Happenings* won't do us very much good.

Generally, daily newspapers have a religion section and a religion editor. We can call the paper and ask for the name of the religion editor so we'll know to whom to send things and whom to call.

Public relations professionals try to get to know their contacts at media offices, so we might want to consider that, too. Why not take the religion editor to lunch? It's a sure way to find out what he or she is looking for, and it certainly can't hurt the chances of getting some coverage.

Newspapers offer a better opportunity for feature

STRATEGY AND TACTICS: THE PLAN TAKES SHAPE

coverage, primarily because they need so much more information every day than magazines. Also, we don't have to be two months early—two days will often do.

A news desk will generally want to assign a writer to cover a story instead of accepting freelance work as magazines do. That's another reason it's a good idea to get to know the religion editor—so we can communicate what's coming up and drop some ideas for potential feature stories.

Daily newspapers usually publish the religion section on Saturdays, and it's probably planned a few days ahead. Ask the section editor about the deadlines.

Newspaper advertising is often much cheaper than magazine advertising, but we'll probably get better results going the free route. This is because people pay more attention to editorial matter than to ads. While we may look to the paper for certain advertising (we want to know what groceries are on special, what stores are having a furniture sale, and so on), we generally pay more attention to editorial space. And the very fact that something is mentioned even in the "community calendar" impresses us as literally a "newsworthy" event.

In addition, since any newspaper advertising we can afford would probably be pretty small, we run the risk of its being overwhelmed in the clutter.

Newspapers give us a few options magazines don't, however. For instance, if we're having a seminar on Christian education, we can call the religion editor, the education editor, and maybe even the city editor. If one of them doesn't think it merits feature coverage, maybe another will. So our chances of getting feature coverage are better. (But if one section editor agrees to do a feature, don't call another; newspapers frown on that.)

Small weekly papers are a different matter. There we may be in touch with the editor or managing editor directly, and that's someone we can get to know personally.

Like magazines but unlike daily papers, weekly newspapers will often accept feature stories from freelance writers. Weeklies will also send a reporter if they sense a story. Weeklies usually don't pay for freelance articles, whereas magazines do. There is no particular reason why. But some weekly papers do pay a token amount for features; better to ask ahead.

Although buying ads in small weekly papers is relatively inexpensive compared to daily newspapers, it still doesn't attract the readership of editorial matter and still can get lost in the clutter.

Besides, our chances of getting some free press in a weekly newspaper are pretty good because the papers are usually pretty starved for good material (as evidenced by the amount of "filler" material they contain).

RADIO

Unless you live in the middle of nowhere, there are probably several radio stations nearby. Look in the Yellow Pages for a listing. As with print media, call the stations and ask for the name of the public affairs director.

You may send the public affairs director a "PSA," which stands for "public service announcement"—radio's version of free advertising. Most stations have a set format of how PSAs should be presented—things such as when and how long. Many will even help write them to match broadcast style.

Most PSAs are either ten or thirty seconds long. It's probably a good idea to send each station a :10 version *and* a :30 version. The easier we make it for the station personnel to run it to fit their scheduling, the better. Chapter 5 explains how to write a PSA.

We can also buy ad space on radio stations. Generally, though, there will be too much waste. Most stations—including top-40, country and western, and news/talk outlets—will buy more people than we need.

If there are one or more Christian stations in the area, we may want to consider buying some time. First, ask the station to send a rate card to see how much commercials, or "spots," cost. Usually, radio spots run sixty seconds, compared with thirty seconds on TV. But other lengths are available, depending on the message.

Be careful: some stations won't air free PSAs if we're buying ads. Their theory is that if we can afford advertising, someone more needy is more entitled to free time. Ask the person at the station about its policies.

If the budget does allow buying radio time, work closely with the station's advertising manager to make sure all their deadlines are met. Radio, fortunately, needs little advance time. In fact, it is possible to provide a script in the morning for the afternoon disc jockey to read live in the afternoon, if need be; but of course, it's always smart to be well ahead of schedule in case any problems arise.

TELEVISION

Television stations also accept PSAs. Call a station to find out its policies. It may have a printed sheet to send you.

Commercial time, even if just run locally, is prohibitively expensive to most church activities; and, even if the time weren't too costly, it's difficult to produce a decent TV commercial for less than $1,000. Most local commercials cost between $5,000 and $50,000 to produce, and national spots can cost ten times that much or more.

Once again, TV is very expensive because of its tremendous waste factor for a small churchwide activity.

Never miss an opportunity, however. PSAs are free, so we should use them as much as we can. Free waste isn't something to worry about!

HANDOUTS/FLYERS

Handouts and flyers should usually be included in our strategy because they're inexpensive to produce (use the church copier or, with bigger budgets, have a printer make them) and inexpensive to distribute (in the church lobby or

Sunday school classes or, if we can find some volunteers, in nearby shopping areas).

Generally, we can double up this medium with direct mail, at least in part. If we plan properly, we can probably use the handout as part of the direct mail package.

A SAMPLE MARKETING PLAN

The media we have surveyed are the ones we are most likely to consider in developing our strategy. Having viewed the media scene, let's walk through another sample marketing plan.

NORTH COAST EVANGELICAL FREE CHURCH CAR WASH MARKETING PLAN

HISTORICAL INFORMATION: We've never had a church car wash before.

OBJECTIVES: Persuade members of the church and community within a five-mile radius of the site to come to have their cars washed.

STRATEGY: Announcements at church, in the bulletin, in the newsletter.
Mailing to members.
Posters.
Press release to newspapers.
PSA to radio stations.
PSA to TV stations.
Handouts/flyers.

TACTICS: Announcements at church/in bulletin July 7, 14, 21, and 28.
Article in the August newsletter.
Mailing to 150 members July 29.
75 posters for distribution in church and local businesses within walking distance of car wash; Rich and Kit to distribute.

STRATEGY AND TACTICS: THE PLAN TAKES SHAPE

Press release to *San Diego Union & Tribune, Escondido Times Advocate, Oceanside Blade-Tribune, Vista Press.*

PSA to KSUZ, KMMT, KESC, KOCN radio (:10 and :30); PSA to KFFM-TV, KFMB-TV, and KSCL (:10 and :30).

150 flyers for Spud and Karen to distribute August 3.

EVALUATION: Set historical with number of cars washed and dollar amount earned.

BUDGET: No budget but office funds to cover all costs.

Strategy

Notice that the strategy did not include magazines; this is because *San Diego* magazine is the only available local publication, and it does not have a calendar section.

Tactics

Let's look at the tactics we recommended based on the strategy.

Announcements at church. The four Sundays preceding an event is usually a pretty good rule of thumb for announcements at church. Before that, it's so far off that people won't get too interested.

Announcements in the bulletin. Four weeks looks pretty good here, too, but that's very subjective. We should just try different methods until we're comfortable with what we think works best in our particular church.

Always try to be in the bulletin and announcements at least two weeks, however. We're all exposed to so much information that sometimes it takes a few times before something clicks.

Newsletter. The August newsletter is mailed the last week in July and the event is the first Saturday in August, so the timing is perfect. The car wash should be fresh in people's minds Saturday morning if they read about it Thursday or Friday.

If we have graphic capabilities for the newsletter, a simple, strong, clear visual (such as a photo or drawing) along with the story might help people remember the car wash. Also, if it's going to be held at a location away from the church, it's a good idea to consider using a map.

Mailing. Try to time this as appropriately as possible. Mailing it on Monday for a Saturday event seems pretty safe—unless we want people to reply first. In that case, we need to mail at least two weeks earlier.

Posters. Posters are an ideal reminder vehicle for this type of event and can help reach the secondary target audience if they're in small business windows near the car wash site.

Newspapers. A press release is sent to local dailies and weeklies. Since several communities (each with its own paper) are nearby, it's a good idea to send releases to papers that might even be a few miles further away.

Magazines. Since no appropriate magazines were found, this marketing plan won't use magazines.

Radio. There are several local stations, so they will all receive both :10 and :30 PSAs for their convenience.

Television. There are several San Diego stations, but North Coast Church is in North San Diego County, which has only one station. Still, since local residents watch San Diego stations and the time is free, waste is not a crucial factor and San Diego stations will be used in addition to the North County station.

Flyers. Since flyers are inexpensive (they can be run on the church copier) and there were some volunteers, it seems

STRATEGY AND TACTICS: THE PLAN TAKES SHAPE

like a good medium to use on the day of the car wash in the immediate area.

Since the marketing plan is divided into several workable, bite-sized components, it doesn't seem intimidating. Moreover, most church events will use pretty much the same marketing plan with just minor modifications. So after the first few times, it's a snap!

Remember: no matter how easy the process may seem to get after the first few times, we must *always* write up the marketing plan. There are just too many ways to get off course if we don't.

5

Writing to Persuade

Because of the nature of the different media we're using, we get to wear three different hats when writing about our event.

We will use *journalism style* for press releases to newspapers, magazines, and newsletters/bulletin articles.

We will use *broadcast style* for PSAs to radio and TV stations.

And we will use *advertising style* for print ads, brochures, posters, and mailers.

THE JIMMY OLSON HAT—JOURNALISM STYLE

There are a few simple rules for writing a good journalism-style story. These are the *inverted pyramid* method and the *5W's*.

The inverted pyramid means the the most important facts are presented with very few details at first, and as the story goes along, more details and less important facts are systematically added. Here's a simple example:

BOSTON -- A local man bit a dog here today.

John Smith, 42, bit the tail of his neighbor's Scottish terrier mix on Copps Hill at 6 a.m. after the dog allegedly barked all night long.

"I just got upset," Smith said, pulling a hair from between his teeth. "I mean, I was trying to sleep, ya know?"

The dog, Fluffy, refused to comment.

"I'm referring all questions to my lawyer," he barked at reporters.

Notice how the inverted pyramid was used:

First paragraph:	Man bit dog in Boston.
Second paragraph:	John Smith was the man. John Smith is 42. The dog is a Scottish terrier mix. It happened on Copps Hill. It happened at 6 A.M. It happened because the dog barked all night long.
Third paragraph:	John Smith said he got upset. John Smith got upset because the barking kept him awake.
Fourth paragraph:	Dog's name is Fluffy. Dog refused to comment.
Fifth paragraph:	Dog got a lawyer.

Look at how many different *facts* are presented—a dozen facts in just a few short, simple sentences. And we're finding out more details as we go.

The first task to writing in good journalism style is to

assimilate as many facts and quotes as possible. Generalities and adjectives are *out*. In journalism style, we present no opinions (unless someone expresses an opinion as part of a quote) and only verifiable facts. As excited as we are about this event, we must remain as objective as possible.

Let's take a list of facts and try to prioritize them in order of importance.

> The event is in Pixley.
> Pixley Community Church is located at 4th and Main.
> The event will happen Saturday evening.
> The event will take place at Pixley Community Church.
> The event is an ice cream social.
> Admission is free.
> It starts at 6 P.M.

What's the most important fact? How about the fact that an ice cream social is taking place?

The story might read something like this:

> An old-time ice cream social is scheduled for this Saturday in Pixley.
> The social, which starts at 6 p.m., will be held at Pixley Community Church. Everyone is welcome, and admission is free.
> The church is located at Fourth and Main Streets.

There are at least eight distinct facts in this story, yet it's only four sentences long. Brevity is important to editors; try to limit a press release to one side of one page, and try not to fill even that entire page. If an editor needs more facts, he can call us. But if we try to present too much information, our press release will probably end up in the wastebasket.

THE FIVE W'S

Journalists sort facts into five categories:

>WHO
>WHAT
>WHEN
>WHERE
>WHY

These are called the 5 W's and, with few exceptions, every news story should have them all within the first few paragraphs.

Let's look back at some of the earlier examples and plug in the 5 W's.

MAN BITES DOG

>*Who?* John Smith.
>*What?* He bit a dog.
>*When?* 6 A.M. today.
>*Where?* Copps Hill in Boston.
>*Why?* The dog made him mad.

If we can not find the answer to all these questions in the first two or three paragraphs of a story, the item needs to be reworked. For instance:

>BOSTON -- A local man bit a dog here.
>John Smith, 42, bit the tail of his neighbor's Scottish terrier mix after the dog allegedly barked all night long.

Something's missing, right? You can probably guess that it happened in the morning in this particular story (because the dog had barked all night long), but when in the morning? And more important, what day—today? Yesterday? Last Thursday?

Let's use another example:

ICE CREAM SOCIAL

Who? Pixley Community Church.
What? They're having an ice cream social.
When? Saturday evening at 6 P.M.
Where? Pixley Community Church, Fourth and Main.
Why? (Not stated.)

Notice that the "who" does not necessarily have to be a *person*. "Who" can be a company, an organization, even a country ("Today the Soviet Union announced . . ."). Notice also that the "who" and the "where" may be partially or completely the same.

Notice also that there's no "why" here. There doesn't always have to be a "why." In this instance, it could have easily been added as a final paragraph:

Pastor David Simcox said his congregation is hoping to show the people of the community ways the church may be able to meet their needs.

So when we're writing a press release or newsletter article about an event, we should follow this formula:

1. Assemble as many facts as possible. Make sure those facts can answer the questions of the 5 W's.

2. Try to put them in order from the most important to the least important.

3. Using only one or two short, simple sentences per paragraph, write a story of no more than a half-dozen paragraphs, or about enough to fill between a half and two-thirds of a double-spaced typewritten page.

Since practice makes perfect, let's use a complete example.

WRITING TO PERSUADE

D. L. Moody Film Series

Who?   Eastside Church.

What?   We're having a D. L. Moody film series, "The Life and Times of D. L. Moody."

When?   September 5, 12, 19, and 26 at 6:30 P.M.

Where?   Eastside Church Auditorium, 335 Occidental Parkway, Portland.

Why?   To expose the community to one of the 19th century's great teachers of Scripture.

Admission will be 75 cents; senior citizens and children under 12 are free.

Popcorn and punch will be served after the films.

"We've been on a waiting list for 3 years to get these films, they're in such demand," said Molly Partridge, Eastside director of education.

Films won a bronze medal at the International Christian Film Festival in 1984.

There are four films:
The first is entitled *D. L. Moody: Boyhood to Manhood.*
The second is *Moody's Early Ministry.*
The third is *Evangelizing England.*
And the fourth is *The Fruits of Moody's Ministry Today.*

(Okay, I cheated; they're already listed pretty much in order of importance here!)
The story might come out something like this:

PORTLAND -- An award-winning film series on the life of nineteenth-century evangelist D. L. Moody is scheduled for four Sunday nights in September at Eastside Church.

"The Life and Times of D. L. Moody" will be shown September 5, 12, 19, and 26 at 6:30 p.m. in the church auditorium at 335 Occidental Parkway.

"We've been on a waiting list for three years to get these films," said education director Molly Partridge. The series, which is in heavy demand, won a bronze medal at the prestigious International Film Festival in 1984.

The film series includes "D. L. Moody: Boyhood to Manhood," "Moody's Early Ministry," "Evangelizing England," and "The Fruit of Moody's Ministry Today."

Admission is 75 cents; children under 12 and senior citizens are free. Popcorn and punch will be served following the films.

Information may be obtained by calling the church office at 555-1212.

That's all it takes. Nothing fancy, just a logical, concise presentation of the facts with no editorializing.

Once we've written and edited our own story, we can add a headline. The editor may change it to suit the paper's style, but it is helpful to him for us to write our own.

To write a headline, look over the first paragraph and trim it down even further. Headlines that would be suitable here are

FILM SERIES TO BE PRESENTED

AWARD-WINNING FILM SERIES COMING TO TOWN

EASTSIDE CHURCH OFFERS FILM FESTIVAL

Always write the headline *after* you've finished the article, because the headline is supposed to summarize—not dictate—the story.

THE WALTER CRONKITE HAT—BROADCAST STYLE

To write PSAs for broadcast media, we follow much the same steps as with the journalism style. The difference is, this time our words are written to be spoken instead of read silently.

Journalism style sounds different from the way anyone speaks—but broadcast style should sound the way we speak. It's more casual, yet there are stringent guidelines.

Since we've already gathered all the facts for our news articles, we don't have to repeat that process here. We can refer to the same fact sheet.

Look over the journalism story. We're just going to rewrite it a little.

The rule of thumb for broadcast style is that the language must be conversational, since someone is going to be reading it aloud. In other words, write it "like you say it."

Look at the news story you've written and ask yourself, "How would I tell a friend about this if he or she were sitting here in the room?"

Let's look at the last example this way:

Journalism Style

An award-winning film series on the life of nineteenth-century evangelist D. L. Moody is scheduled for four Sunday nights in September at Eastside Church.

Now, people don't usually talk that way, so for a spoken message we adopt broadcast style.

Broadcast Style

There's going to be an award-winning film series at Eastside Church this month. It's all about the life of D. L. Moody, one of the great evangelists of the last century.

At this point we ought to take note of the time limitations we'll have on the air. In the marketing plan we probably planned for a ten-second PSA and a thirty-second PSA. That's a pretty short message.

Review the broadcast-style paragraph above. Time yourself as you read it aloud. Make sure you read it so slowly that you think you ought to be reading it faster.

How long did it take? That paragraph probably took seven or eight seconds—leaving you just enough time to include a phone number.

There's going to be an award-winning film series at Eastside Church this month. It's all about the life of D. L. Moody, one of the great evangelists of the last century. For more information, call 555-1212.

There! That's your ten-second PSA.
To write the longer version, start with the first part and continue—but remember to move the telephone number to the end.

There's going to be an award-winning film series at Eastside Church this month. It's all about the life of D. L. Moody, one of the great evangelists of the last century.
The four films will be shown Sunday nights at 6:30 p.m. Admission will be seventy-five cents, but seniors and kids can attend free. The church will provide popcorn and punch after each showing.
The series is called "The Life and Times of D. L. Moody," and it won a bronze medal at the 1984 International Film Festival.
For more information, you can call the Eastside Church office at 555-1212. That number again, 555-1212.

We don't need to write a headline for a PSA; but we will need to identify it briefly. The next chapter will explain how to do this.

THE GRAY FLANNEL HAT—ADVERTISING STYLE

Believe it or not, there are some strict guidelines for writing advertising copy.
That may not seem to be the case, considering all the different kinds of ads we see these days. The reason is twofold.

First, the "rules" governing advertising copy are usually strategic, so we don't necessarily see them reflected in the finished ad.

Second, many ads today break the rules! Suffice it to say that "rule breaking" in advertising should only be attempted after mastering the basics and years of objective and subjective research and testing as to what's effective.

Fortunately, ads that stick to the fundamental guidelines we're about to look at are consistently effective—and sometimes even more effective than ads that we might think did better.

The first rule to remember for writing ads—whether it's the components of a mail package, a flyer, or a newspaper ad—is that trying to be creative can be the worst thing to do!

That's right! Sometimes the most "creative" ads are the least successful in selling a product or promoting interest in an event.

One leading adman tells of several test situations where this was proven to be true. In each instance, people were asked which of several ads they liked best. And in every situation, the ads the people said they liked were not as effective as the ones they didn't like as much.

Why is this? One reason is that most of us are pretty resistant to intimidation or the "hard sell." We complain about all the "dumb TV commercials" and "junk mail" we have to put up with. So an ad that's particularly clever or creative is just that—a clever or creative ad.

On the other hand, an ad that is purely informational and not too exciting often comes across most effectively. If we're interested in what an ad has to say, we're open to considering the product or service offered.

That's why we see a lot of printed ads that look like articles and have the word ADVERTISEMENT across the top. Even though we know it's an ad, we're subconsciously prone to take it more seriously because it seems more objective.

Strangely enough, many of the ads—particularly TV

commercials—that come to mind as outstanding award-winners also had a *negative* impact on sales.

What makes a good ad? It must relate personally to the people seeing it and promise a benefit to them.

FEATURES AND BENEFITS

The only reason anybody ever buys anything is because it'll do something for him or her. We buy soap because we need to keep clean. We buy a car because we have to get around. We go to a show because we like to be entertained.

For that reason, our advertising copy should promise the reader what he or she will get out of our event. Now, promoting Christian activity is admittedly a little different, since we're often asking for support or commitments, but generally, this is the case.

For instance, why would people want to come to our Teen Life meeting? What are they going to get out of it? Fellowship? A chance to grow closer to the Lord? Fun?

These are all *benefits* of the event. They are quite different from *features*, and we have to be very careful to notice the distinction.

The features of a product or event are its characteristics. A shiny new bike may have a chrome-spoked derailleur. So what? Nobody is going to buy that bike because of a feature like that. But the benefit of a chrome-spoked derailleur is that we don't have to pedal as much. Now, there's a benefit for me—in fact, that may even make me decide to buy that bike.

The features of our event include things like "John MacGibbon will be speaking on personal devotions" and "We want to raise $5,000."

Our job is to turn those features into benefits. I may not care that John MacGibbon is speaking on personal devotions, but I'd surely respond to "Find out how to draw closer to the Lord—day by day." And I certainly am not happy about putting money into the collection plate, but I could appreciate your asking me to "Be a part of the bus-team dream" or "For your $25, two children will have an opportunity to hear the gospel in our city."

Make a list of the three main benefits of your event. Sometimes there will be more, other times there will be less. Use the most important one as your creative foundation.

If we try to stress more than one benefit, we may end up giving a confusing message. Key in on the first, then throw in the others as additional support later on instead of giving equal emphasis to all three.

Often the major benefit is inherent in the event. For instance, if we're having a good old-fashioned hayride, it's pretty obvious that the benefit is fun and fellowship. So we don't have to go too far and talk about fun and fellowship first and then mention a hayride; we put the hayride up front. Just use common sense and what appeals to *you*.

One of the legendary greats of advertising called this "reason-why" copy. Give the target audience as many "reasons why" as possible to take us up on our offer.

HEADLINES

Unlike journalism style and broadcast style, in advertising we write the headline first. The most successful headlines are generally informational or news related:

> INTRODUCING A SUBCOMPACT
> FOR PEOPLE OVER 6'4"!

> BAKE PIES WITH THE FLAKIEST CRUST EVER

> ANNOUNCING A DRAIN CLEANER
> THAT'S SAFE AROUND CHILDREN!

Let's take a few sample Christian events and try to write headlines for them.

EVENT:	Church rummage sale.
MAJOR BENEFIT:	Good things cheap.
HEADLINE IDEAS:	GET GOOD THINGS CHEAP
	HOUSEHOLD ITEMS—UP TO 75% SAVINGS!
	HOW TO GET $20 OF STUFF FOR $1.75

Admittedly, none of these headlines is outstandingly "creative," yet each communicates helpful, benefit-oriented information to the target audience.

It's hard to go wrong when using a "How to . . ." headline. So unless we can come up with one we (and several other people) think is much stronger in terms of communicating the main benefit, it'd be a good idea to use "How to . . ." heads most of the time.

Other consistent winners include "Why (fill in target audience) should do something" or "Why (target audience) will benefit from something" or "Five ways something can do something."

No matter what, never use a period at the end of a headline, even if the grammarian in you winces. A period says to the eye, "Stop!" whereas you don't want the reader to stop, but to read on.

Here's another neat trick: put quotation marks around the headline. That's because studies show that otherwise identical ads—one with quotes around the headline and the other without—get different results. The ads with the quotes generally reap about 10 percent more responses than the ads without the quotes. Most likely, that's because of the human interest appeal of quotes—they suggest there's a person involved instead of a faceless advertisement.

Or better still, use a quote as a headline, if you can get a good one. Like this:

"I GOT A $20 LAMP FOR 79 CENTS AT THE CHURCH RUMMAGE SALE LAST YEAR"

THE BODY COPY

The words that appear after the headline are called "body copy." Body copy offers us the opportunity to persuade others to come to our event.

To write the best copy possible, think in terms of you and one other person in a room. The other person is a member of your target audience. Think about how that person thinks, feels, and acts. How would you go about persuading him or her to do what you want?

Use the words "you" and "your" a lot. As with broadcast style, use conversational language. ("Wouldn't you feel great knowing your $10 put us over the top?")

And don't be afraid of using fairly long copy. But if you do, remember two things: (1) don't expect many people to read every word, yet (2) there's a way to tell people what you want without their *having* to read every word.

NESTLING

"Nestling" involves harboring a few subheadlines, or "subheads," into a long block of copy. People will tend to scan the subheads, so we should write as if it were a copy block all by itself. For example:

HEADLINE: Announcing a new seminar series designed especially for Christian educators

SUBHEAD: The author of *Give Us This Day Our Daily Chalk* tells how to get the most out of students

SUBHEAD: He'll explain his "7 steps to involving parents"

SUBHEAD: You'll discover methods of motivating even the most difficult students

SUBHEAD: He'll give you ideas on making homework a joy

SUBHEAD: And you'll keep the prized seminar notebook

   This technique allows us to catch two different kinds of people within our target audience.
   First, it provides an outline to write the copy itself—a good platform to persuade people who *do* read every word. And it makes *writing* the copy much easier, because it's as if we're writing a few short sections instead of one long, intimidating one.
   Second, it grabs the scanners. If they "cheat" and just scan the subheads, they'll get all the information we want them to get. Yet we have the credibility that long copy adds. It seems that even if people don't *read* long copy, it reassures them that we have something worthwhile to say and offer to them.
   Having said all that, I believe that since we are not professional advertising copywriters, we'll probably be better off using just short copy in most of the pieces we produce. Short copy is fine. Long copy is fine. Don't ever sit down and say, "This ad will have long copy" or "This ad won't." Use as many words as it takes to tell the story in a persuasive, informative fashion.
   Use short sentences and paragraphs; keep the words simple. Our mission is clear, effective communication. The more complex and technical the writing, the more difficult it is to understand. Think about how *you* react to something that's easy to follow compared with something that uses many big words and long sentences.
   Don't try to impress anyone with cleverness or flowery language, either. Anything that distracts from the message—even technique—should be avoided! Give plenty of facts, and the more specific, the better. Generally speaking, avoid generalities!

THE CALL TO ACTION

Have you ever read a letter or an ad that wanted you to do something but left you confused and frustrated as to how to do it?

Always ask your target audience to do something, and always make it crystal clear exactly what you want them to do. This is called, quite simply, the "call to action," and it appears near the end of the ad.

Here are some examples of good, solid calls to action:

Return the enclosed card along with a check for $10 to . . .

Sign up in the lobby after church Sunday morning.

Bring your cake to room 21-B Saturday between 3 and 4 p.m.

Clear, isn't it! There should be no question in anyone's mind as to what he or she is supposed to do.

DEADLINES

If we're asking people to do anything besides come at the appointed hour, we should specify a deadline or cutoff date. If there isn't really a deadline, create an artificial one. More people will respond if there's a date than if it's left open—that's the way people are.

Please return the form to the church office no later than Friday, November 12.

To make sure your spot is reserved, please give your $5 deposit to Charlie by Sunday after church.

REPETITION

Repetition is a device used by lots of good teachers because it takes several times before something clicks.

Repetition is a device used by smart advertising copywriters, too. Change the wording slightly, but repeat key points (like the benefits and important dates) throughout the copy.

WRITING THE COPY

Now that we have all our facts assembled in order of importance, have listed the most important benefits, and have written a great headline, we're ready to write the copy.

Don't be intimidated. Just send up a prayer and start writing your message the way you'd say it. And stop when you've said everything you think you need to say to persuade someone to attend.

If you've written subheads, that should make things fairly easy. Just tie in your copy with the subhead that came right before it, write a paragraph or two, lead into the next subhead, and repeat the process. Here's an example:

HEADLINE: "Why you should consider the all-church retreat"

COPY: Have you ever been in the mountains with a group of Christians? If you have, you know what an awesome, powerful impact a spiritual retreat can have on your walk with the Lord.

The First Church of Bentley is having its second annual all-church retreat at Mt. Buckhorn next month, and it's an experience you and your whole family will not want to miss.

SUBHEAD: No missing work or taking valuable vacation time

COPY: This year's retreat will be held during the three-day July 4th weekend, so you won't have to miss work or use up any vacation time you may already have planned. We've taken extra care to schedule plenty of growth-oriented sessions as well as plenty of recreation to make this a time of growth and fellowship your family will always cherish.

SUBHEAD: Carl Sotheby to speak on "core growth"

COPY: Several speakers will attend the retreat. Among them is Carl Sotheby, the church's missionary to Tannu Touva. Carl will give his famous "core growth" talk on personal spiritual development.
Other speakers will include Pastor David Grey, Associate Pastor Bejma Ali, and a special surprise guest.

SUBHEAD: Unlimited outdoor fun for the whole family

COPY: During free times, your family will have numerous activities to choose from. Things like boating on nearby Lake Tanganyika, fishing on the Makinak River, hiking, picnics, or just relaxing under the tall fir trees.

SUBHEAD: A limited number of cabins are available

COPY: Unfortunately, there are only 12 cabins available to us, and each can house 4 families. That means we can only accept reservations from the first 48 families.
To guarantee your family a retreat they'll never forget, fill out the enclosed card and send it along with the $10 reservation fee to:

>   Mabel Hilkey
>   Buckhorn Retreat
>   First Church of Bentley
>   1211 Main Road
>   Bentley, Alaska 97889

Make your reservation by Friday, May 27, to ensure your family a spot. The total cost will be $35 per family, which includes 8 meals and 3 nights lodging.

That's an example of long copy—but then again, there's a lot to tell. Notice how the copy and subheads work together to create a persuasive presentation of facts. There's very little editorializing. It doesn't say, "This is a great retreat; you'll have a fantastic time!" Instead, it presents facts that imply those benefits, so the target audience, we hope, reaches those conclusions on their own.

The next step after actually writing the copy is to edit it. In editing, be merciless—cut more than you really want to. The purpose of this editing is to "tighten up" the copy by getting rid of adjectives, extraneous material, and unimportant facts. This should make the second draft more readable and inviting than the first.

If you're writing short copy with no subheads, make an outline (as if you were using subheads) before you start. Something like this:

OUTLINE

HEADLINE: "Why you should consider the all-church retreat"

POINTS:
1. No missing work or vacation time
2. Carl Sotheby to speak
3. Recreation
4. Few cabins available
5. Call to action

Notice that the outline matches the subheads of the long-copy example. Here's how the copy might read:

HEADLINE: "Why you should consider the all-church retreat"

COPY: The First Church of Bentley is having its second annual all-church retreat at Mt. Buckhorn next month, and there are several reasons you'll want your family to attend.

First of all, you won't have to miss work or use any extra vacation time because it's over the three-day July 4th weekend.

Not only that, Carl Sotheby, the church missionary to Tannou Touva, will give his acclaimed "core growth" talk. And Pastors Grey and Ali will speak—not to mention the special surprise guest.

While not at the sessions, you'll be able to enjoy boating on Lake Tanganyika, fishing on the Makinak, hiking, picnicking, and relaxing under tall firs.

The trouble is, there are only 48 spaces available. To guarantee your family a spot, send the enclosed card and $10 reservation fee to:

Mabel Hilkey
Buckhorn Retreat
First Church of Bentley
1211 Main Road
Bentley, Alaska 97889

Make your reservation by Friday, May 27. The total cost will be $35 per family, including 8 meals and 3 nights lodging.

This copy is less than half as long as the original, yet it communicates several important, persuasive benefits. And it also demonstrates the power of editing.

There's an old adage in advertising, "The more you tell, the more you sell." That's a pretty sound rule of thumb, within reason. So in this case, we should use the longer version if we have the space. If we don't, we just keep on paring down until we can squeeze in as much information as possible in the space allowed.

If space is limited, here's how to trim some more:

HEADLINE: "Why you should consider the all-church retreat"

COPY: The First Church of Bentley is having its second annual all-church retreat at Mt. Buckhorn next month. Highlights include:
- Missionary Carl Sotheby to speak on "core growth"
- Pastors Grey and Ali also to speak
- A special surprise guest
- Boating, fishing, hiking, picnicking

Only 48 spots are available, so send the card plus $10 reservation to:

    Mabel Hilkey
    Buckhorn Retreat
    First Church of Bentley
    1211 Main Road
    Bentley, Alaska 97889

Reply by Friday, May 27. Cost is $35/family, including 8 meals and 3 nights lodging.

How about that? We cut it almost in half again, but it still tells the story. Not as strongly as the other two versions, yet it does the job if space is limited.

Since what we say is the most important element of our advertising, we will generally use the length of copy needed to determine how the layout of the ad looks instead of the other way around. The next chapter will explain how to make the design and the words work together.

But before we turn to design, we should review our marketing plan again. Does this copy meet our objectives? Does it fit into the strategy? If not, we must fine tune here.

If all looks good in matching and fulfilling our marketing plan, it's time to break out the crayons.

6

Designing to Persuade

As with writing, our designing and presenting the material will fall into the different categories of press releases, PSAs, and advertising.

With each, the overall purpose of design is to create interest by being visually appealing. That's not as hard as it sounds, especially if we follow some time-proven guidelines.

JOURNALISM STYLE—THE PRESS RELEASE

Journalists like to use standard formats to keep things simple for them and for typesetters. (Typesetters take the typewritten copy and set it into the nice, neat columns you see in newspapers and magazines. That will be covered in chapter 8.)

Always use standard 8½" x 11" paper. We should use our church or group letterhead or, better still, have special letterhead made with the words *PRESS RELEASE* printed across the top in bold, capital letters. If we send out more than two or three press releases a year, it's worth considering because it isn't *too* expensive.

If there's an artist or graphic designer who'll donate the time, he or she may take a few hours to design some press release stationery. If not, local printers are usually able to help. Often we can just add the words in an appropriate spot on our existing letterhead.

TYPING THE PRESS RELEASE

In the upper right corner, type the words FOR IMMEDIATE RELEASE in all capital letters on one line and underline them. On the next line, write CONTACT: followed by the name of the person who can answer questions and provide more information. And on the third line, put the appropriate phone number. The material should look something like this:

<u>FOR IMMEDIATE RELEASE</u>
CONTACT: Charlene Coler
(909) 555-1212

Skip a few spaces, then type the headline in one long line across the page. Don't divide it up into different lines, and if it takes more than one line, try to shorten it. Use all capitals again, and underline them.

<u>MISSIONARY TO PRESENT TALK ON NEW GUINEA</u>

<u>EAST BEND CHURCH NAMES NEW PASTOR</u>

<u>TEEN CAR WASH TO HELP NEEDY SATURDAY</u>

If the headline is fairly short, think about whether you've given enough information; if you think it's all right, that's fine—it doesn't have to extend clear across the page.

To type the release in a journalism format, set your typewriter margins on 10 and 70 to create a sixty-character line. Try not to go over sixty characters, even if this means leaving a line noticeably short. Editors prefer to receive copy this way, with substantial margins.

Always type the copy double-space. That's so they can insert proofreaders' marks and edit as they see fit.

Indent all paragraphs five spaces. For the first paragraph, type the city you're writing from (called the "dateline") in all capitals, followed by a space, two dashes, another space, and then the lead sentence.

The copy should look like this:

```
ALBUQUERQUE -- One of the nation's top Christian

educators will speak at Cross and Candle High School's

commencement next week.

    George Thornton, a professor of theological seman-

tics at Mariemont College, will address the convocation

on the subject "The Christian Student: College as a

Mission Field."
```

If the release absolutely, positively requires a second page, put

-more-

at the bottom right corner of the first page.

For the second page, use a plain white sheet or, if you have one, a "second sheet" piece of your group's letterhead.

At the top left corner of page 2, type a key word or two from the headline (journalese: a "slug"), followed by ADD 1. It should look like this:

EDUCATOR SPEAKS
ADD 1

When the story is finished, put the symbol

-30-

centered two or three lines after the last line of the story, not at the bottom of the page. This is a proofreader's symbol indicating the story is finished.

Here's how the entire press release should be typed:

<u>FOR IMMEDIATE RELEASE</u>
CONTACT: Kathy Jewett
(717) 555-1212

<u>BAKE SALE TO BENEFIT NURSING HOME PATIENTS</u>

MT. WASHINGTON -- Proceeds from a bake sale this Saturday will be donated to the Oregon Hill Nursing Home.

The sale, sponsored by Evendale Community Church, will be held at the church parking lot at 927 Brown Street from 9 a.m. to 6 p.m. Saturday, April 17.

"We're hoping for a turnout like we had last year," said church spokesman Finan Dandy. "Last year we were able to give over $750 to the home."

Cakes, cookies, pies and homemade candies will be available, and judges will award the best-tasting cake as a door prize.

In the event of inclement weather, the sale will be moved into the church auditorium.

For more information, call Kathy Jewett at 555-1212.

-30-

Notice that the name and number of the person to contact is given in the story for people who read the article in the paper, while the name and number are provided at the top for the editor's easy reference.

BROADCAST FORMAT—THE PSA

We can use church letterhead for the PSA too or, better still, press release stationery.
Put the same information in the upper right corner, but add the length and an identifier that this is a PSA:

:10 PSA
FOR IMMEDIATE RELEASE
CONTACT: Kathy Jewett
(717) 555-1212

Use a headline again, but this time it serves more to identify the subject matter to the announcer, since the headline won't be read over the air.
Broadcast style uses *triple* spacing for easier reading:

There's going to be a bake sale this Saturday, and all

the proceeds will go to a local nursing home.

The sale will be held at the Evendale Community

Church parking lot from nine to six.

For more information, call 555-1212.

If it's at all possible, try to help out the person who'll be reading the announcement. You can do this by spelling out certain phrases (notice "nine to six" instead of "9–6" in the above example), because some common ways of abbreviating things get confusing when you're trying to read it aloud. Write "Kansas" instead of "KS," "Road" instead of "Rd.," and "October" instead of "Oct."

Also, spell out difficult names phonetically. For example, if we mention Barb Covell, we can write it like this:

The study will be led by Barb Covell (CO-vul), an

elementary school teacher from El Paso, Texas.

End the copy with the mark

###

centered, two or three lines after the last line of the copy. (Broadcasters don't use the -30- symbol to avoid confusion about the copy length.) Here's how the PSA should be typed:

:30 PSA
FOR IMMEDIATE RELEASE
CONTACT: Herman Hintz
(212) 555-1111

GANGSTER-TURNED-PASTOR TO TELL STORY FRIDAY

DAYTON -- A former gangster who's now a pastor will tell his story here Friday evening.

Scarface Murphy, now a Baptist minister in Tampa, Florida, will talk about his former life—and his new life—at the First Missionary Alliance Temple on the north side Friday at 7 p.m.

Admission is free, and anyone who's interested is welcome to come and hear this unique testimony.

Murphy will autograph copies of his new book, "Guns to God," in the lobby after his lecture.

For more information, call Herman Hintz at 555-1111. That's 555-1111.

For both press releases and PSAs, it's better to load the copy machine with letterhead and copy onto that paper than to type the release onto letterhead and run copies of the whole thing. So if we can run copies directly onto letterhead, type the copy onto a white sheet of paper with a sheet of letterhead behind it on the typewriter to see how it fits. That way we can photocopy the original directly onto letterhead.

Unless it's absolutely unavoidable, never send a press release or PSA on plain paper—it looks quite unprofessional. Editors are easily persuaded by how professionally releases and PSAs are done. A sharp, well-done piece may get airtime or printed space over another piece that isn't done as well—even though both are equally important.

ADVERTISING DESIGN

With rare exception, the only media we'll use that require advertising copy are posters, handouts and flyers, and direct mail.

Since the same format often can be used interchangeably for those media, we'll treat them all similarly.

It's interesting to note that the same format also can be applied to newspaper and magazine advertising—just about everything but radio and TV.

What we're doing when designing to persuade is taking advantage of how the human eye moves over an ad and helping the target audience along.

EYE MOVEMENT PATTERNS

Studies show that when looking at a printed page, people tend to notice things in this order:

1. Artwork (photography or illustration)
2. Headline
3. Copy

Smart advertisers know that since we're creatures of habit, it's best to take advantage of those habits. For that reason, since we go from top to bottom and then left to right in Western culture, a solid layout might look like this:

1. Artwork across the top
2. Headline down below
3. Copy below the headline

The headline is by far the most important element of an ad, so never, ever go without one. We can, in rare instances where space is limited but long copy is necessary, go without artwork—just using a headline and copy will do.

The length of copy will usually dictate the size and shape (horizontal, vertical, or square) given to the artwork.

If we have short copy, the artwork will cover about two-thirds of the page, which, if it's on an 8½" x 11" sheet, is roughly a square.

For long copy, however, we will leave about one-third of the page for the artwork, which means it must fill a horizontal space. That puts an additional consideration on what to use for artwork.

SELECTING ARTWORK TO COMPLEMENT THE MAIN BENEFIT

Let's look at the headline. That's our primary resource for what should go into the artwork.

Here are some sample headlines, followed by some ideas of what the artwork should be:

HEADLINE: How to help your kids get the most out of school

ARTWORK IDEAS:
Parents laughing with child; books open
Bored-looking child staring into space in classroom
View from behind of child running to school

Notice that two of these are positive images and one is negative. It's generally better to use a positive image, but a negative image can imply, "This is your problem, and we have a solution for it." Any of these ideas can work, as long as we relate them to the copy.

Here's another sample:

HEADLINE: Why Darien Free Church *desperately* needs a new van

ARTWORK IDEAS: Empty pews
Old van in poor condition—should be exaggerated
Closeup of child's face

These all seem as if they'd work fairly well because of dramatic impact. Experiment a little—don't just go with your first idea. Discuss ideas with other people.

The crucial point to remember about artwork is, it must *not* create a conflicting message with the headline. The two should work together to communicate a simple idea—presumably, the major benefit to the target audience.

CAPTIONS

For some reason we all love to read captions. In fact, captions below photos or illustrations are usually the second-most-read part of an ad—after the headline. Always include captions, and always get the main benefit into them.

TYPE

We should always run the copy in black ink on a white or a light, off-white background. Do not run type in colors, and never "reverse" type, which means using white letters on a black or other dark-colored background. Type set that way is difficult to read.

The whole purpose of designing an ad is to communicate a message as effectively as possible. We're used to black type against white backgrounds—that's how all newspapers and magazines do it—so anything else is difficult to read. Never do anything that will make communication more difficult.

Another characteristic that we're used to is *serifs* on type. Serifs are the tiny little "feet" on the ends of letters; our eyes tend to latch onto the serifs so we can read the letters more quickly and easily.

Also, use upper- and lowercase for headlines, captions, and copy in advertising—don't use all capitals. Type set all in capitals is harder to read because the letters don't have little up and down ridges (like the bottom of a g or a j) of lowercase letters—which our eyes subconsciously catch to make reading easier. (The reason we use all caps on press release headlines is for emphasis, assuming the editor is reading the material; plus, that's the format editors are used to. But when we want someone to pay attention to our ad, we should use upper- and lowercase.)

We'll examine type in more detail in chapter 8, which deals with printing.

THE PENCIL LAYOUT

Once we know roughly how much space our copy will take (more on that in a minute), we make a pencil layout. That's a rough design of what the ad will look like, done in pencil for easy changing and erasing.

This procedure basically enables us to see how much space each element will take up in the final ad. We use 8½" x 11" paper (if that's the size the final piece will be), make a box where the art will go, scribble in the headline, and make a few horizontal lines to represent the copy.

If we can afford to have the type set professionally, we should take our pencil layout along with the copy to give the typesetter a general idea how the copy should come out.

If you've never worked with a typesetter or printer before, ask around for a good recommendation or simply call a few from the Yellow Pages and ask for a price quote on the specifics of the job you're doing. This also will be treated in more detail in chapter 8.

If we can't afford to have type set, we must prepare it ourselves on a typewriter to fit the layout. This might entail some trial and error. A few things to remember:

1. Since this is an ad, not copy to be edited, type it single-space. However, if you have the room, it's helpful to the eye to use paragraph space, which simply means double-space between paragraphs only.

2. Don't worry about having even margins on both the left and the right. Your typewriter will "justify" the left side, but it's perfectly acceptable to leave the right side "ragged." Many ads, magazines, and even some newspapers use a ragged-right style now. In fact, it's really easier to read copy that's justified on the left and ragged on the right than copy that's justified on both sides with funny spacing between words to make the lines even.

3. On an 8½" x 11" ad, use two columns of copy instead of one wide one. A single, wide column is difficult for the eye to follow all the way across the page. Three columns will most likely be too narrow and make it difficult for the reader to concentrate.

4. Another good idea is to reduce the size of the type. In other words, if you type the copy on a standard typewriter, it may not all fit or may take up too much space. Photocopy shops usually have machines with reduction features, so you can reduce the size of your copy for only five or ten cents! If you want to try this, remember to type it proportionally larger than the space it's going to occupy.

5. Indent all paragraphs—the eye likes to catch that little bit of white space, and it helps move the reader along.

Here's how to do the headline if you can't afford a typesetter: use *rubdown lettering*.

Rubdown lettering is a wonderful invention that's available in most stationery stores. It consists of filmy sheets containing the letters of the alphabet, numbers, and other symbols. When the desired letter or symbol is placed against a sheet of paper and rubbed over the top, the character is transferred onto the page, comparable to the way designs are transferred by an iron to a tee-shirt.

A sheet of rubdown type costs around a dollar, so you should be able to invest in one or two. Each sheet should have enough letters to use it more than once or twice.

A variety of typefaces is available in rubdown lettering, but always use the same typeface for an ad. Don't mix up typefaces, because that creates a jumbled, confusing, busy look. Pick a type style that's easy to read, preferably one with serifs. Avoid script, thin lettering, or any style that isn't simple and plain. The job of the headline is to get itself read—so it should be as easy to read as possible.

PRODUCING THE ARTWORK

Generally, a photograph is more effective than a drawing—but some subjects may require a drawing because there's really no way to represent the message in a photo.

Unless we're going to print the ads in full color, use black-and-white film to take the pictures; they reproduce better.

As with other parts of creating ads, try to find a volunteer with professional experience to take the photos.

Carefully plan what you want the photo to communicate so you can just set up the shot, take it, and proceed. If they're not carefully planned, photo sessions tend to drag on and on and on.

Try to find someone who has access to darkroom equipment. That can save money.

If we have a good quality black-and-white photo with sharp images and good contrast, we may be able to get away with photocopying our ads if there's no money in the till.

If we have about twenty dollars to spend, we can take the photo to a printer and ask for a *halftone*. A halftone is a photographic image made up of little dots for better reproduction quality. Halftone images show up better on photocopies than photos do, and they must be used if we're having our ad printed.

FLYERS AND BROCHURES

So far we've been looking at an ad that stands as a poster or, folded, as an insert sheet in a mailing.

If we want to make a little flyer that opens like a mini-booklet and is printed on both sides, we should follow some guidelines.

First, the simplest way to develop a brochure is to use a sheet of 8½" x 11" paper, folded twice to form three sections (like a letter). That's what people are used to, so the method won't detract from the message.

Second, there are several steps involved in preparing an appropriate cover. When using the standard two-fold format, we have two options for the cover design: vertical or horizontal.

The vertical design is probably more common but often harder to use, since a headline may have to be stacked on several lines instead of running straight across.

As with a full-page layout, place the artwork at the top and the headline below. We probably won't have any copy on the cover.

The inside gets a little tricky, since there's a back flap folded over, too. The best way to handle this is as a separate item, usually as the response coupon. That way we can use the two inside panels on the left for our information.

If we use this format, we can make an inside subhead go across the top of those two panels with copy with perhaps additional artwork—including the captions—below.

The extra panel on the right can have the space for the target audience to fill in name and address.

If we use the horizontal format, we may want to try something different—like putting the headline on the cover, the artwork on the extra inside flap, and the copy inside.

We should take plenty of time beforehand to make several pencil layouts when preparing this kind of brochure, for as you can see, it can get rather confusing. We must use plenty of paper and make as many mock-up versions as it takes until we're satisfied that we've got a design that communicates our message intelligently and effectively.

Put the church or group's logo (if there is one), name, address, and phone number on the back panel at the bottom. That's an important point—make sure the church's address and phone number are on everything we put together! That can help us avoid some embarrassing situations.

The next chapter will provide some hints on copy and layout as they apply to the very specialized discipline of direct mail.

7
The Mail: Our Secret Weapon

Direct mail is a multi-billion dollar business in the United States and one of the fastest-growing forms of marketing ever to exist.

It's a great way to get a complete message to a very specific target audience—ideal for many Christian projects.

Virtually all the mailings we receive fall into one of two formats: self-mailers and the "classic" package.

SELF-MAILERS

Self-mailers are just that: a folded piece that includes the address and postage on the outside and the message all over. The whole "package" consists of just one large piece of paper, or several pages forming one mini-newspaper or booklet. It is distinguished from a brochure only in the fact that it is designed for mailing in itself.

Self-mailers usually don't generate as many responses as the "classic" format for a variety of reasons. Primarily, it looks less personal and more like "junk mail."

A specific time when a self-mailer can be more cost-effective than a classic mailer is when we're doing an extremely high-volume mass-mailing—say, to every household in the San Francisco Bay Area, which amounts to hundreds of thousands.

Our mailings will most likely be limited to a few hundred or more, so it's better to avoid self-mailers as much as possible.

But if we do have to use a self-mailer—when we want to do a mailing but can't even afford to use envelopes—be sure to plan accordingly when doing the layout. If we're using an 8½" x 11" sheet, we probably want to fold it like a letter, staple the end, and put the address and postage on a third of one side of the sheet. So we must leave that space blank (except for the return address) when we're putting the mailer together.

Postcards also fall into the self-mailer category and can sometimes be quite effective if we have a short message. But the more information we can send, the better off we usually will be.

THE "CLASSIC" PACKAGE

The "classic" package consists of a business-size envelope that houses a cover letter, brochure, "publisher's note," and reply device. The reply device may be either a reply card or a reply card/form with a reply envelope.

Sometimes, if there's enough in the budget, there's also an involvement device.

Let's look at each part of the classic package.

OUTER ENVELOPE

Don't ignore the outer envelope—it's one of the most important components of any direct-mail package.

The outer envelope's primary purpose is *to get opened*. It becomes more important now that it does more than carry around the goods, doesn't it?

Since the outer envelope's purpose is to get opened, there must be some devices to help accomplish that feat.

First of all, use a standard, business-size envelope—what's called a "Number 10." Number 10s seem to get opened more than other sizes. The reason? We've heard it before. It looks more personal—like a letter. We like getting letters, but we don't like getting junk mail.

Use your church or group stationery. It would help if it's off-white. Envelopes with a slightly different color seem to attract more notice.

Advertisers often put a "teaser" headline on the outside of the envelope, but we'll probably be better off just letting the church letterhead speak for itself. People don't want their church being too "pitchy," so clean and professional is best.

However, if we're having an event that emphasizes fun (such as a spring carnival or a hayride), we may want to consider a teaser headline on the outside of the envelope. Just use good judgment and common sense based on the "personality" of your group, the target audience, and the event.

We should keep any headlines straight and simple:

INSIDE: INFORMATION ON THE FALL HAYRIDE!

TEEN LIFE WANTS YOU TO HAVE CLEAN HUBCAPS!

IT'S CHURCH COOKOUT TIME!

And remember, their wording should entice the reader to rip that envelope open.

The quantity of the mailing may dictate use of an outside headline, too. If we're mailing two dozen, we can do it by hand, but if we're mailing 1,500 . . . Also, printers often don't want to print onto an envelope that's already made. They do the printing before the envelope is turned into an envelope—so we may have to custom-order envelopes if we want to use a headline.

THE MAIL: OUR SECRET WEAPON

Moral of the story: don't worry about headlines on envelopes.

When addressing, avoid using labels if possible. The best way to boost interest is to type each person's name and address on the outside of the envelope. If we have a word processor or computerized typewriter that can do this, terrific! Personalization is the key. If there's a label on the envelope, I know I'm just a number to you, not a person.

With all this talk of personalization, you might think handwritten addresses work best. Surprise! Typewritten addresses usually work better than handwritten. No clear reason why—they just do. Type does look more professional than handwriting, of course.

Most Christian groups can qualify for nonprofit organization postal rates, which are substantially lower than first-class rates. If you can't get nonprofit rates for some reason, contact your postmaster about bulk rate. You'd be surprised at the minimum identical pieces you have to mail to qualify—just a few hundred. That will save you some money. Also, using a meter instead of a stamp shouldn't hinder response. Most people don't seem to think about that difference anymore.

The next chapter will deal more with the different options the post office provides and several ways we may be able to get reduced postage costs.

THE COVER LETTER

The cover letter is perhaps the most crucial component of a direct-mail package and should always be included. In fact, if we can't afford much, we should forget the other items and just send a well-worded letter.

The letter should be personalized too, if that's possible. If our group doesn't have a typewriter with a memory function, we might seek access to one—it really makes a mailing a lot more attractive. And boosts response.

Always start with a salutation, just like a "real"

business letter. Use the person's name, but if you can't personalize, make it singular. In other words, don't say

Dear Friends

   or

Dear Sunday School Teachers

   but instead say

Dear Friend

   or

Dear Member

We're writing to one person, and one person is reading the letter at a time.

Always indent paragraphs, and use single-space within paragraphs. Use double-space between paragraphs. This keeps it looking light and easier to read.

People tend to scan letters, so we should put our main message in the letter three times: at the beginning, at the end, and in the postscript. *Always* use a P.S. It's the second-most-read part of the letter.

In fact, use the P.S. to your advantage by repeating the main benefit and the "offer" there—summarize your event. Here are some examples:

P.S.   Don't forget, you must return the card by Friday, October 25, to guarantee yourself a spot in the cults workshop.

P.S.   If homemade apple pie, chocolate cake, and fresh-baked cookies sound good to you, be sure to come early to the bake sale this Saturday.

P.S.   Remember, the Matthew study group is only open to the first 10 people who sign up—so act now!

Use your church letterhead, and type the letter in black

using upper- and lowercase. But don't be afraid to underline key words or CAPITALIZE words or phrases you want to emphasize.

We should sign each letter in blue ink or, for larger quantities, see about having it printed in blue—it's not that expensive. The next chapter will talk more about printing.

If we need to use more than one page, we can either go onto the back side or a second sheet. A second sheet looks more professional and realistic, but of course it costs more.

If we spill over onto a second page, we should finish the first page mid-sentence or mid-word if possible. This will help entice the person to continue reading.

DON'T DO THIS: After they've been made, the quilts will be loaded into vans where they'll be taken to the Sunshine Store.

over, please

DO THIS: After they've been made, the quilts will be loaded into vans where

over, please

If we use more than one page, some subheads in all capitals, underlined, will help break up a long block of copy.

Also, don't be afraid to use bullets for a list.

- Bullets are graphically appealing;
- They highlight key items;
- They're an ideal method to use for lists;
- Scanners tend to read them.

When typing, we can make bullets by using a small o and filling it in with a black pen, or we can use the plus sign (+) or asterisks (*). I think big black dots look best.

THE BROCHURE

The two previous chapters have provided sufficient information for preparing brochures. Just be sure the brochure ties in well with the other components of the direct-mail package.

THE "PUBLISHER'S NOTE"

The publisher's note got its name because years ago, publishers included it in their mail-order packages. It's simply a small piece of paper that shouts, "Hey!" and gives the mailer one last chance to appeal to the customer.

You've probably seen them in some mailings you've received. They usually have what looks like a handwritten note saying, "If you don't read anything else, read this" or "Before you say no, read this."

Publisher's notes usually increase response about 10 percent compared with occasions when they're not used.

Usually they're on a half sheet of 8½" x 11" paper and then folded over once.

It's a good spot for a real-person testimonial—which is always a strong motivator.

Here's an example of a publisher's note:

COVER: "I got more out of the Baker Brothers seminar
(handwritten) than I would have thought possible!"

HEADLINE: Look what people are saying about the Baker
(inside) Brothers seminar

COPY: "I almost didn't end up going, but I'm sure glad I did. I got more out of the Baker Brothers seminar than I would have thought possible!"

Mrs. Gracie Smothers
Altoona, PA

> "The Baker Brothers seminar turned my life around. They gave me new insights into walking with the Lord I didn't think were possible."
>
> Mr. Theo Brooks
> Eugene, OR

> "Thank you, guys! May the Lord richly bless you for all the great work you're doing."
>
> Mrs. Chris Carringham
> Denver, CO

If we can get a few different people to say nice things, that's probably the best bet. But if we can only get one, that's still powerful and effective.

If possible, have the publisher's note printed on paper that's a different color from the rest of the package. Blue is usually a good choice. A publisher's note is simple to do and inexpensive, because we can do it on a photocopy machine and make two from every sheet of paper.

THE REPLY DEVICE

If we're asking someone to send money, we must always use a reply envelope along with a reply card/order form. If we're not asking the target audience to send anything except a reservation card or some other information, a reply card will do—unless we're asking for some personal information.

Should we pay the postage on reply mail? Probably not. Generally, including postage will increase response a little, but we're in a special situation. People understand that Christian groups are not usually endowed with great sums of money and high budgets, plus we're really not selling something like a business. For church mailings, the extra response, if any, due to our paying the postage usually won't justify the cost.

If we're not including postage, we *must* include a

stamp-sized square on the upper-right portion of the card or envelope containing the words "Place Postage Here."

Always self-address the reply card or envelope. And always include the whole offer—including places, times, and dates—on the reply form. The reply device should be a mini-ad in itself, reiterating all the important information the target audience needs to know.

Leave plenty of space for the person's name and address. Do it this way:

Name _____
Address _____
City _____ State _____ Zip _____
Phone (____)_____

Always fill out a sample form before it is printed up, because you may find that one line or another is too short or too cramped, or even that you're missing a line.

INVOLVEMENT DEVICES

Involvement devices are neat little things designed to get hands moving—because if their hands are moving, your prospects are more likely to send in a reply.

Little tokens, stamps, and stickers are common involvement devices. If you've ever received a "sweepstakes" mailing, you know how extensively they're used.

Unfortunately, custom-making such items and including them usually cost too much for church mailings. But don't give up all hope. There are plenty of things to be done with a little creative thought.

For instance, we can buy brightly colored round stickers at stationery stores, design a reply device with a place to stick a "yes" response, and include the stickers in the mailing.

If we have the time and the money, involvement devices are a good idea because they almost always increase response.

THE WHOLE PACKAGE

It may surprise you, but we should be able to mail all the items in the classic package for just the basic postal rate. We can get a lot into that first half-ounce the post office allows.

When putting it all into the envelope, don't fold things up together so they can be easily pulled out in one clump. Put each piece in separately. That way the people will be more prone to look at each piece individually—and if we've worked a powerfully persuasive message onto each, we have a better chance of convincing them to attend, sign up, or whatever.

3–D MAILINGS

The only mailings that consistently outperform the classic package are 3–D mailings: boxes.

The trouble is, these are prohibitively expensive. They're worthwhile for our purposes only if we're mailing a few pieces—perhaps up to ten—and can afford to spend two or three dollars on each.

For instance, a church wanted to entice a certain Christian singer to perform at an annual event they were staging. They sent him a three-part mailing that consisted of a heart-shaped box of candy, a tiny "LOVE" sculpture, and finally a personal letter explaining the church's desire.

To heighten the impact, the church didn't identify itself in the first two mailings. That little element of mystery and surprise made the mailing even more irresistible.

A mailing like that can be very effective—and lots of fun—when the right circumstances present themselves.

8
Getting It Printed and Mailed

Chapter 6 talked about artwork and touched on preparing artwork for reproduction. This chapter will begin where that one left off.

Depending on our budget, we'll most likely photocopy our material or have it printed offset. Let's take a look at these two methods.

PHOTOCOPYING

Using photocopies gets the job done, but if there's any way we can afford printing, we should have our materials printed. The added quality should boost our response tremendously—usually more than enough to justify the expense.

But if we're dealing with a very low number—a few hundred pieces or less—or there's simply *no* money—we have to work with what's at hand. The redeeming factor is that photocopying technology is well-advanced and the equipment available today does a good job.

We can use the basic design principles from chapter 6 to create an attractive, forceful ad on a photocopier. And it's easy to do.

THE LAYOUT

Once we've done a rough layout and written the copy, we're all ready to create the *final art*. Final art is simply the master or original from which we make copies.

If we're not having the piece printed offset, it's probably a safe bet that we're not having the type set, either. So our only realistic option is to type the copy right onto the layout.

Use scratch paper to see how the copy will fit. If you're using 8½" × 11" paper vertically, use two columns across the bottom and don't try to justify the columns—leave them ragged on the right side. Indent paragraphs, type the copy single-space, and use a paragraph space if there's room.

When you're happy with how it looks, type it onto a blank sheet of white paper, which will become your final art.

Leave a half-inch margin at the bottom and about three-quarter-inch margins on both the right and left sides.

When the copy is all neatly in place, use rubdown lettering for the headline. The length of the headline will determine the size of the letters to use.

Type size is measured by *points*, with 72 points to the inch. The size of a letter is measured from the top of an ascender (as in a *b*) or capital letter to the bottom of a descender (as in a *y*); thus a capital letter in 36-point type is actually about 30 points, or a little less than a half-inch high.

Generally, if we're using an 8½" x 11" sheet, 30-point, 36-point, or 48-point will be the best sizes to use. If we have a pretty short headline—less than five or six words—it's okay to use 48-point. If there are no more than a dozen words, 36-point would probably be best. And for long headlines, a dozen or more words, use 30-point.

These rules are flexible, of course. As we do more and more ads, we get a good feel for what works best.

Use upper- and lowercase, not all capitals. Don't use a period. Use quotes if possible.

To make sure the letters line up evenly, make a straight black line on a separate sheet of paper and put it underneath the sheet you're using for final art. That makes a good base line for the letters, so words don't go floating up or down.

The space that remains is for the artwork.

Leave ample margins all around; if we were having the material printed, we could *bleed* the art off the edges, but that doesn't work very well on photocopy machines.

Don't forget to type in the caption. Plan this as you did the copy. Be careful—rubdown lettering has been known to come off in a typewriter! (If it does, you can fill in damaged spots carefully with a very-fine-point black pen or pull the letter off with Scotch tape and try again.)

If we're using a photo, it *may* reproduce reasonably well if it's sharp, clear, and black and white. Color photos don't usually copy as well. If we can afford a few dollars for a photographer or printer to make a halftone, that helps.

Apply the photo or other illustration with a tiny amount of rubber cement, wax, or a Gluestick. Don't tape anything down. Make sure there's nothing on the sheet that isn't black. Few colors reproduce well on a photocopier; most turn into a nondescript grey. Be careful—even writing from a black ballpoint pen doesn't usually reproduce well. Blue tends to disappear most easily. Try to avoid "cutting and pasting" as much as possible; that tends to leave unwanted shadows and lines on photocopies.

If we have the time and energy to add a little color after our illustrations are copied, we can use a felt pen to fill in some areas as desired. For instance, if there is a church logo at the bottom, we may want to shade it a little bit. But that usually detracts attention from more important elements, so it is good to use a second color sparingly, if at all. Exercise judgment and remember, sometimes ornateness detracts from communicating a simple message.

You can copy onto colored paper if you want; in fact, an off-white stock is usually a helpful attention-getter. Avoid bright or gaudy colors—they make things hard to read. Use white, creams, light blues, or perhaps light greens or yellows. Light red, unfortunately, appears pink, which doesn't please some people.

For letters, always use white paper unless the stationery is a different color. If there's time, add a signature with blue felt pen on each.

When using a mimeograph machine instead of a photocopier, apply the same basic principles along with a little common sense.

OFFSET PRINTING

Offset printing, a shortened term for the offset lithography process, is the method that most small print shops recommend for printing our materials. Some churches own offset presses.

For more than a few hundred copies, offset is almost always cheaper than photocopying. The more we print, the cheaper each copy becomes, because the biggest part of the cost is the initial setup incurred by the printer.

When printing offset, a printer has to make a photographic plate of the final art from which the finished material is actually printed. If that costs $20, that means one copy costs $20; the first 500 cost $20 plus 2 cents each (which averages to 6 cents each), yet 1,000 cost $20 plus $20 (or 4 cents each), and 10,000 cost only a fraction over 2 cents each.

If the church has an offset press, all well and good. If not, ask for recommendations on local print shops. Otherwise you will simply have to start calling at random from listings under "Printers" in the Yellow Pages.

Before we call, we'll have a written outline of what we want so we can ask for a job estimate. You'll be amazed at how widely the estimates vary among printers for the very same job. We'll need to tell the printer something like this:

I need a job estimate. I'll need 1,000 copies, offset, on 8½" x 11" uncoated bond, one color, one side, no bleed. I have camera-ready art. What will the cost be? What about the turn-around time?

Here's some of what we said: The "uncoated bond" is the kind of paper we want; coated paper is slick and shiny, and uncoated is not. Most typing paper is uncoated. Bond is a good kind of paper to use, and in fact, most typing paper is bond.

"Turn-around time" is printer's jargon for how long the task requires.

Usually we will want to go to the printer who gives us the lowest bid. But always consider the quality of his work either from our own experience or from samples of other jobs he's performed.

When using a printer for the first time, it's always a good idea to visit the shop in person unannounced and to ask to see a few samples of work that are similar to what you want.

PREPARING CAMERA-READY ART

Preparing camera-ready art for a printer is a little more demanding than producing final art for photocopying.

If we're preparing camera-ready art, we'll need to have the type set, have halftones made from photos, and be reasonably proficient at pasteup.

TYPESETTING

If we can afford to use a printer, we'll have to have our type set, which makes an ad look much more professional.

Take your copy to a printer along with a rough layout and tell him the type needs to be set. We'll need to *spec* the type, which is short for "specify." The items that should be specified are type size, leading, and typeface.

The printer can suggest an appropriate type size, based on the length of copy and the layout. Eight-point, 9-point, and 10-point are pretty standard for body copy and easy to read. Often a typesetter will set the type in two or three different sizes at no additional cost and let us choose which fits best. Now that typesetting is primarily computerized, having it set in different sizes is just a matter of pressing a button or two.

Generally, leading (pronounced "LED-ing," not "LEED-ing") isn't a problem. Leading is how much space there is between lines of type. It got its name years ago when printers actually put thin bars of lead between the metallic slugs of type. But today most type is generated by computer.

There is a standard leading that typesetters use for body copy, and they'll use the standard leading unless we specify otherwise. It's probably best just to let them use the standard leading and not worry about it.

We will want to select a traditional, easy-to-read typeface. Select one with serifs. Usually, if you don't specify, the printer will select a standard typeface for you anyway. But be sure to mention it, because more and more typesetters are using faces without serifs—nice to look at, but harder to read. Printers have books full of different typefaces—believe it or not, there are hundreds of them—but most would rarely be used for body copy. As a point of interest you might note that the body typeface for this book is Melior; certain extracts are set in American Typewriter; and the "display headings" (chapter titles, for example) are set in Benquiat.

HALFTONES

If we're using a photo in our publicity material, we'll need to have a halftone made. A halftone, you'll recall from chapter 6, is an image of the photo that is made up of many tiny dots for the ink to adhere to in the printing process. The beauty of having a halftone is that we can change the size of the photo to suit our needs.

Since we have a layout, we know how big we want the finished halftone to be. For example, if we have a 3" x 5" photo and the area in the ad is 4½" x 7½", the halftone can be reproduced at 150 percent (100 percent being actual size).

We can enlarge the photo even more if we want to eliminate portions of the photo and focus on a specific area. This is called *cropping*. When cropping, measure the part of the photo you want and treat that as the actual photo size.

For example, suppose we have a 3" x 5" photo, but we want to use only a part in the middle that is 2" x 3". The area for the photo on the layout is 4" x 6". Therefore we'll have a halftone made at 200 percent and then we'll crop the area we want onto the layout.

Don't cut the photograph itself. Rather, take the entire photo to the printer, explain what area you want to use, and show the printer how big the final picture should be. He or she will take it from there.

PASTEUP

When we have received everything from the printer—the set type and the halftone—it's time to produce the final art, also called camera-ready art or the *pasteup*.

Here's good news: you can mark on the pasteup with a light blue pencil or a light blue felt-tip pen, and it won't show on the printed piece! That should make doing the pasteup a little easier. (When the printer is ready to print the piece, he actually takes a photograph of the final art—but light blue doesn't show up). Press very lightly, or some shadows may appear in the printed piece.

The best way to produce camera-ready art is to use heavy white paper or even card material. Make a very fine, light blue outline of the finished size you want—probably 8½" x 11". This will be your working area.

Next, make light borders for where your copy and art will go—about a half-inch on the bottom, a half to three-quarters of an inch on the sides, and a half-inch on the top.

Or, if the work will be printed offset, we can *bleed* the photo off the top and sides this time, which has an appealing look. That means we bring the edge of the halftone all the way to the edge of the 8½" x 11" border and beyond on top and the sides. Go a little over the edge ("bleed" it) to avoid an accidental white border; the printing process will take care of the extra. If you plan to bleed the photo, allow an eighth-inch more area for the halftone both vertically and horizontally than your layout calls for.

If you're not doing a bleed, however, adhere to the margins suggested. You want to have either a good-sized margin or none at all—a skinny or uneven margin doesn't look attractive.

For pasting up the type, many printers will actually set the type to match our requirements if we provide them with a rough layout. That way, we just lay down the type (remember, it's computer-generated onto paper, not metal bars) in one or two large pieces instead of having to worry about lots of cutting and pasting and uneven lines. Be sure to ask if the printer can set the type to match the layout.

Of course, a printer can do the headline, too, so we won't have to use rubdown lettering.

The printer may wax the back of the halftone and copy so that they stick to the layout page. If this was not done, we can use rubber cement, a Gluestick, or wax to make everything stay down tight. Just be sure everything is where you want it before you press it down. Never use tape.

Once the work looks finished, run a photocopy to see if everything is straight. Don't worry if cut lines show or if the overall quality of photocopy isn't good; final art often lacks crispness on the photocopier that it achieves when printed.

COLORS

If there is a really good reason to use a second color, we will need to make an *overlay*. An overlay shows where the second color will go. It's a clear plastic-like sheet that's taped on one side and acts as a flap over the layout. On the flap, there's a cutout shape of the area that will have the second color.

Unless we have an artist helping us or a printer who's willing to go the extra mile, a second color is difficult to use well. The problem is that the color must hit the intended spot exactly on the printed page or it looks awful. So use a second color sparingly unless you have professional help.

FULL COLOR

Full-color printing is called *four-color* or *process color*. The names derive from the fact that all the colors of the rainbow—and many in between—can be derived by combining two or more of the four basic colors in varying degrees: red, blue, yellow, and black. The technique is quite expensive unless we're going to have a print run of well over a thousand pieces.

The main cost factor lies in the setup. A *separation* is a negative that provides one specific basic color for later combination with the negatives of the other colors. A printer or photo laboratory has to make four separations to create the final negative. That can cost several hundred dollars, all before anything has been printed. So even if we print a thousand sheets, we pay about a dollar per sheet compared with just a few pennies for one color (black ink).

If we have a big budget and print several thousand pieces, however, it's worth the extra expense in most cases. Four-color pieces almost always achieve much higher response rates than one-color ads. If we have a promotion we think is worthy of four-color and we have the budget, we can call a color separator (ask the printer for a recommendation) and talk about what needs to be done. Primarily we'll need to modify our camera-ready art a little and, of course, have top-quality photography or artwork. And if we're going four-color, we'll most likely want to use coated stock to bring out fully the beauty of the color.

TIME

When the printer gives us a cost estimate, he or she will also tell us how long the project should take. Of course, for an additional fee he can probably speed things up a bit, but that gets expensive and can strain a relationship if we ask for "miracles" all the time.

Usually, simple one-color jobs take a few days, although quick-print shops can do them in just a few hours. Just be aware that we can't always count on having something *now*—so be prepared several days or even weeks in advance if possible. It never hurts to have our materials in hand a little early.

In fact, each time we do a project, we should discuss a tentative *production schedule* with the printer. It should include things like this:

FINISH ROUGH ART/COPY	May 7
FINAL ART TO PRINTER	May 11
MATERIAL FINISHED/STUFFED	May 15
MATERIAL MAILED	May 17
EVENT	May 31

MAILING

You should be able to get nonprofit group rates; call the local post office to find out. If there's some reason you can't, look into bulk-rate mailings. It may save you only a few pennies on each copy, but in a mailing of a thousand pieces, the savings could be substantial. And you may be surprised at how few pieces you actually have to send to qualify for bulk rate—as low as two hundred in many cases.

Presorting by zip code or carrier route can save money, too. Ask your postmaster about ways you can save—each mailing is different.

Also find out about permits—a necessity if we want to use business reply envelopes or business reply cards.

When stuffing a direct-mail package with all the

components mentioned in chapter 7, avoid the temptation to fold them all together into one neat little clump. Studies show that you'll increase response by inserting each piece in the envelope separately. People will tend to spend a few seconds with each separate piece, and one big batch may not get as much attention.

LISTS

Professional marketers buy or rent lists of names for mailings; but you already have your list. If you have a huge budget and want to do a mailing to a highly targeted group, contact a list broker. You can get a list such as "Lawyers in Lane County" for about fifty dollars per thousand names. Look under "Mailing Lists" in the Yellow Pages.

WHEN TO MAIL

Assuming you're mailing everything locally, count on about 2–3 days for the letter to arrive. Take note: that's true for first class and third class for local mailings, except during the Christmas season. Locally, third class doesn't necessarily take any longer, even though it can cost less.

Mail the letters one-to-two weeks before the event if it's a one-time mailing without a reply device.

If you want a reply of some kind, make the mailing about two weeks before the reply deadline set on the copy. Try to make the reply date the last Friday of the month; it can be from two-to-four weeks before the event itself.

If you're doing more than one mailing about the same event, space them about two weeks apart. Example: If the seminar is to be held on October 17, send the first mailing September 16 with the reply device needed by Friday, September 27. Do the follow-up mailing (one version to people who said yes, another to people who did not respond) around October 5.

After mailings, you may want to make follow-up phone calls. Chapter 9 has some hints on this.

9
The Follow-up

Now that the mailing's out, the press release and PSAs are sent, and the posters are up, we can rest easy. Right?

On the contrary, now it's time for one of the most important steps—the follow-up.

Always follow up press releases and PSAs with a phone call a few days after you've mailed them. Budget enough time for the letter to arrive and then a couple of more days to make sure the person had a chance to read it.

Identify yourself and say you wanted to make sure the person got the press release or PSA. This is a good time to ask if he or she has any questions or needs more information. This contact can often be the difference between being forgotten and getting some press.

TELEMARKETING

As for the target audience to whom you mailed a packet, call them, too. This is called *telemarketing*, and it is a great way to raise the response levels.

Prepare a script, or at least an outline, of what you want to say. Outlines are better because the person making the call doesn't sound so stiff. We've all received calls where the person on the other end is obviously reading a script, and it isn't too impressive.

Keep an accurate list of who's been reached and their response; there's nothing worse than doubling up and making the same call twice! And be sensitive about *when* you call—not too early or late in the day.

FULFILLMENT

The other component of follow-up, loosely called *fulfillment*, generally includes recording an order and sending the product that has been purchased. In our case, though, there most likely won't be a product; but there will often be a reply card, reservation form, or a check to take care of.

Always note the date you receive a reply *right on* the reply. Make a list of names, addresses, and phone numbers of people who respond; they're the best "prospects" for your next mailing.

To obtain historical data for future mailings, you may want to make a simple graph showing how many responses you got each day in relation to when you mailed the packages.

If the responses are coming to the church office, make sure you've left instructions with everyone who might handle the mail. It's an easy oversight to make, but could cause a lot of trouble. Make sure there's good communication as to who's responsible for doing what. A box or mail slot specifically labeled "Picnic Replies" or "Seminar Reservations" is helpful.

Also, make sure there's a typed-up fact sheet handy in case someone calls to ask for more information. In short, brief the staff well.

When all the responses are in, make a count of how

many came in by phone, how many by mail, and how many by other methods (like the collection plate). Total them up and calculate your response rates for each medium as well as an overall response rate.

For instance, if we mailed 1,200 letters and received a total of 34 reservations, we had a response rate of 2.8 percent. Pretty low? Actually that may be a very good response rate. It seems logical that if we do a good mailing to a good list of people, we would get *most* of them back. Strangely enough, more will probably end up *unopened* than *responded to*. And the vast majority of people will simply not respond. Try to relate this to how you respond to mailings: don't you toss more than you respond to?

Highly successful direct-mail programs done by major advertising agencies will often pull 2 percent or 1 percent or even less—and still be profitable! So don't worry if only a handful comes back; the fact that people responded to a mailing at all shows you did a lot of things right!

Then again, church mailings do have the advantage of audience interest, so the response rate could run above 10 percent.

EVALUATION

Now that the results are in, it's time to evaluate in light of the marketing plan. (You have been checking it occasionally all along, haven't you?)

Compare your results with the criteria you set. Did you achieve them? Did you surpass them? If so, how? If not, where do you think things went wrong?

Write a very brief—maybe one page—report on how the objectives were met. This will become your historical information for next year. It's easy to put it off, but try not to—you'll regret it next time you do a similar program. And if you wait too long, you may forget some important details.

10
Newsletters and Brochures

If we're doing a newsletter and have some brochures about our church or group, we can apply some of these same principles to these publications to improve them, too.

The most important point is, use them. Communicating your message is the objective, so communicate. Regularly. Often. And in a manner that's clear and memorable.

NEWSLETTERS

A good way to get a feel for what our church or group wants and needs from a newsletter is to do some simple research—ask them! Perhaps the best way to do this is through a bulletin insert. Include a small questionnaire, provide pencils, and ask people to return them in the collection plate that very day. Ask questions such as the following:

- How often do you look at the church newsletter? Every issue ____ Most issues ____ Some issues ____ Rarely ____ Never ____

- Do you read every article carefully? _____ Skim? _____
- What is your favorite section? _____
- Your least favorite? _____
- What would you like to see included that isn't?
  _____
  _____

- Do you think the newsletter should come out more often? _____ Less often? _____ It's just about right? _____
- Any additional comments, questions, or suggestions:
  _____
  _____

By keeping most questions limited to checking a box, we're more likely to receive responses, primarily because it doesn't take long for someone to complete the activity.

That's objective research. We also need some subjective research. Ask around. But be sure to ask a wide range of persons—old, young, men, women—not just close friends. Friends tend to share our opinions and may lack objectivity; we want to know any *other* options available.

Once we have reviewed the findings, we should have some pretty good guidelines as to how to proceed.

FREQUENCY

A newsletter can come out weekly, biweekly, monthly, quarterly, or any other frequency we choose. It depends mostly on how much there is to tell, how much we can afford, and how much time someone can devote to producing a newsletter.

Once a month generally works well. Simply choose the timetable that's right for your particular situation. And be committed to sticking with a schedule once you've set one; if you decide to have an issue every two weeks but just can't keep up, change to once a month and do it well. It is better to change midstream and keep on schedule than to have a constant frustration from tyrannical deadlines.

FORMAT

Start "collecting" newsletters from other churches and other groups to see what you like and what you don't like. Make your newsletter a combination of the features you like the best.

A vital point to remember about newsletters is consistency. We're creatures of habit, and newspaper and magazine publishers know this as well as anyone. Think of your three favorite things in the newspaper each day. Don't you pretty well know where to find each one without looking at the index?

Sports news is in its own section. The editorial pages are the last two inside pages of another section. The weather is in a little box where it always is.

People regard periodicals as old friends in a way. We like things to have a feeling of continuity about them. So produce your newsletter with this in mind. Make things easy to find, and make the overall "feel" of the newsletter the same from issue to issue.

Pick a good name and stick with it. Run it the same way every time. Use the same size paper. Use the same typeface for body copy and headlines.

It's okay to change colors and the number of pages if we wish.

To get an overall "look" initially, have someone with a little design ability develop a *format* layout.

A format is just that—an overall example of how pages should look and where things should be. For instance, if we're using 8½" x 11" paper, we can have two or three columns (two is probably better). We can run the page numbers and other identification at the top or the bottom. (Look at a newspaper and several magazines—newspapers usually put this at the top; magazines, the bottom.) We should leave a space for the address or leave it off and plan to use envelopes. These are all matters of format.

One good way to highlight important notices is with standard labels, such as "Music," "Youth," or "Calendar."

We can have these boxed or otherwise called out (as with a second color), so scanners can easily find the things that interest them the most.

Within this format, of course, each issue will change as specific sections grow and shrink, depending on what's happening at the time. Regular features may not even have any news in a particular issue. So although we do have a format, it doesn't get boring by being too much the same each time.

Size is up to us to decide, also. That's a good thing to ask about. Do people like one big sheet that folds up, or several smaller pages? There's no "right" size—whatever meets our needs best is good.

GATHERING INFORMATION

A good editor doesn't write all the news himself—he delegates. Here's a simple trick to having the people most involved with a ministry write their sections without too much pain.

Personally inform everyone you would like their help, and emphasize it will take only five minutes or less of their time once a month. And stress that it will really help them communicate to the people to whom they want to minister.

Prepare a sheet of paper that says something like this:

Please write a sentence or two for the next newsletter about what's going on in your area of concern. Please return this completed form to my mailbox by noon Friday, April 17. Thanks, Marge.

Then make five lines across the page. This makes the task appear so easy, whereas if we had have said, "I need an article for the newsletter by Friday," that prospect would have seemed impossible—and might have ended up being ignored.

Be sure to indicate a deadline date. Recall from our

explanation of direct-mail copy that people tend to put things off without a specific deadline.

Photocopy this sheet onto colored paper. Make the deadline date one week before yours. That way, you can get more information if there's some feature material in their area of concern this time. Plus, that helps you out in case someone *else* misses *their* deadline.

Remember consistency when editing. Don't say "P.M." in one story and "p.m." in the next. Be extra careful about spelling people's names. There may be one misspelling in the whole newsletter, but if it's Charliee's name, you can be sure he'll spot it.

It's helpful to refer to a style manual such as the *Associated Press* (AP) *Style Book* or the *Zondervan Manual of Style*, which are available at many bookstores. They give professional guidelines for numbers ("one" rather than "1"), dates ("Nov. 3", not November 3rd), and many other nuances you probably wouldn't think of but are confusing when you come across them in copy and have to make a quick decision on usage. Note that the AP style book would be a little more journalistic, or a little freer, in style.

BROCHURES

Many congregations have several different brochures about their church and special ministries within the church. There may be a brochure for Mother's Day Out, one for opportunities for service, and so on.

These brochures need a format, too, so they look as if they go together. To get an idea of how good (or bad) formatted brochures can look, go to the biggest two or three banks in your area and take a sample of each brochure. See how they all work together—or, if they're not formatted, how they create a confusing hodgepodge.

Simple design elements can make a good brochure format. Consider a bold line running across the bottom, one inch from the end of the paper, with the headline in the same typeface on each, a half-inch from the top.

See what an artist can do. Ask for a few rough sketches from someone else, or just do a very simple one yourself. Sometimes the simplest formats are the nicest looking.

Even photocopied brochures can benefit from formatting. So if there's no money to print them up with a slick appearance, at least get a cohesive look. Remember the lessons of newsletters: consistency is important in creating a positive, overall effect.

11

Some Final Advice

The best way to make sure our project is a tremendous success? First Thessalonians 5:17: "Pray continually."

Pray that everyone involved will have a right motivation and a right attitude. Pray that the Lord will give us great ideas. Pray that the results He produced will be "immeasurably more than all we ask or imagine" (Eph. 3:20).

And make sure we have lots of prayer support, too. "Where two or three come together in my name . . ."

Ask people to pray that the Lord would use us as a blessing in this instance.

On the more physical level, don't be afraid to ask lots of questions. Printers, typesetters, newspaper reporters and editors, and television/radio news staff are very helpful if we approach them and ask for help.

Also, we must always stick to our plan! That, of course, means we have to have a plan. A road map of written objectives is crucial to achieving positive results.

Finally, remember that practice makes . . . better. Advertising is a unique combination of art and science. If

SOME FINAL ADVICE

we follow some basic principles, we improve our chances of success. If we do a few other things, we can doom ourselves to failure. But the bottom line is, publicity is a very subjective matter and even after many years in the business, many professionals still rely tremendously on personal judgment, common sense, and instincts to make a final decision. (But *only* after they've done a tremendous amount of research, preparation, and planning, which they have followed to the letter.)

So don't be afraid of making mistakes. We all make them. The secret is being able to learn from them so we do a little better next time. If we're not making mistakes, that only means we're not trying innovative approaches to solve problems.

The first appendix summarizes almost all the material we've covered in an actual case history that worked wonders. After that, there are some "fill-in-the-blank" pages to help you get started on the next advertising project you undertake. The book ends with a glossary of terms for handy reference.

Work hard. And have fun.

APPENDIX 1
Case Study: Seminar on Moral Development of Children

This is the actual advertising and public relations program that took place at the Church at the Crossing in Indianapolis in early 1985. It will be outlined step-by-step in the sequence indicated in the chapters of this book.

1. **Prayer**

2. **The Marketing Plan** (completed Nov. 1, 1984)

HISTORICAL INFORMATION: This is the first event of its kind here, so there is no historical information.

OBJECTIVES:

Persuade parents and other interested individuals within the church community to attend the Parent Enrichment Seminar Thursday evening, Feb. 21.

Persuade educators, ministers, health-care professionals, and psychologists within a five-mile radius of the church to attend the half-day workshop Friday, Feb. 22.

STRATEGY:

ANNOUNCEMENTS AT CHURCH will be made.
THE CHURCH BULLETIN will be used.
THE CHURCH NEWSLETTER will be used.
DIRECT MAIL will be used.

A CASE STUDY

POSTERS will be used.
PRESS RELEASES will be mailed to newspapers and magazines.
PSAs will be sent to radio and TV stations.
HANDOUTS will be used.

TACTICS:

ANNOUNCEMENTS AT CHURCH will be made Sunday mornings and evenings Jan. 27, Feb. 3, 10, and 17 as well as Wednesday evenings Jan. 30, Feb. 6, 13, and 20.

THE CHURCH BULLETIN will include mention of both events Jan. 27, Feb. 3, 10, and 17; a separate insert sheet will be included Feb. 10 and 17, including a response device.

THE CHURCH NEWSLETTER will feature both events in the Feb. 1 and 15 issues.

DIRECT MAIL will be used as follows:

    Mailing A to 300 church members
    Mailing B to 300 professionals

POSTERS will be used in the lobby and distributed to local schools as permitted.

PRESS RELEASES will be mailed to the following newspapers and magazines:

NEWSPAPERS

INDIANAPOLIS STAR	Morning
INDIANAPOLIS NEWS	Evening
307 N. Pennsylvania St.	633–9273
Indianapolis, IN 46206	
INDY'S CHILD	Monthly
8900 Keystone Crossing	843–1494
Indianapolis, IN 46240	
TOPICS NEWSPAPERS, INC.	Weekly
	Cynthia Hutt, editor

9615 College Avenue
Indianapolis, IN 46280

844-3311

MISCELLANEOUS

THE CRITERION
P.O. Box 174
Indianapolis, IN 46206

Weekly
Rev. Thomas Widner
635-4531

CHURCH MILITANT
1100 W. 42nd Street
Indianapolis, IN 46208

Monthly
Rev. Edward Berckman
(Episcopal Diocese of Indianapolis)
926-5454

FEDERATION
FORECAST
1100 W. 42nd Street
Indianapolis, IN 46208

Dec. 20, Feb. 20, Apr. 20
Richard Davies
(Church Federation of Greater Indianapolis)
926-5371

PASTOR'S NEWS
NOTES
1100 W. 42nd Street
Indianapolis, IN 46208

Monthly
Richard Davies
926-5371

INDIANA JEWISH POST
& OPINION
611 N. Park Avenue
Indianapolis, IN 46204

Weekly
Betsy Sheldon
634-1307

THE HOOSIER UNITED
METHODIST
1100 W. 42nd Street
Indianapolis, IN 46208

Newman Cryer
(United Methodist Communications)
924-1321

INDIANAPOLIS
WOMAN
P.O. Box 20272
Indianapolis, IN 46220

Monthly
Linda Eder/Connie Rosenthal
547-1993/546-9393

STATE DEPT.
OF EDUCATION
NEWSLETTER

Issue on Feb. 15
Carol Wilkerson
Publications Division
229 State House
Indianapolis, IN 46204-2798

A CASE STUDY

PSAs will be mailed to these TV and radio stations:

TELEVISION	CONTACT/POTENTIAL SHOWS
WISH-TV / CH 8 / CBS P.O. BOX 7088 Indianapolis, IN 46207 924-4381	Hallie Crombaugh INDY TODAY Janice Sharp BEHIND THE SCENES Hal Riceman THIS IS YOUR CITY (Jaycees) PSAs—use form
WRTV / CH 6 / ABC 1330 N. Meridian St. Indianapolis, IN 46206 635-9788	Judy Waugh NEWSMAKERS (w/Howard Caldwell) Tom Brown IMPACT: INDIANA (546-2537) PSAs—use form
WTHR / CH 13 / NBC 1000 N. Meridian St. Indianapolis, IN 46204 636-1313	Pat Chappell INDIANA ILLUSTRATED, INFOCENTER 13 Paul Page SPECIAL SEGMENT PRIME TIME PSAs—use form
WTTV / CH 4 / Local 3490 Bluff Road Indianapolis, IN 46217 787-2211	Joseph Logsdon JIM GERARD SHOW Rich Green YOUR SHOW Chuck Workman FOCUS
WFYI / CH 20 / PBS 1401 N. Meridian St. Indianapolis, IN 46202 636-2020	INDIANA PRIME TIME: Tuesdays: "Trends" consumer, health, education (host Sally Larvick, producer Terri Bowman) Wednesdays: "Magazine" public affairs, producer Kathy Miller
WHMB / CH 40 / Christian P O Box 50250 Indianapolis, IN 46250 773-5050	Orville P. Jones PSAs—use form
WPDS / CH 59 / Local 1440 N. Meridian St. Indianapolis, IN 46202 632-5900	John H. Newcomb, Station Mgr. PSAs—use form

AMERICAN CABLE-
VISION OF INDPLS
3030 Roosevelt Avenue
Indianapolis, IN 46218
632-2288

Jim Magee, program operations coordinator
PSAs to programming dept.

INDIANAPOLIS
CABLEVISION CO. LTD.
5330 E. 65th St.
Indianapolis, IN 46250
353-2225

"Swap shop channel" to :120

RADIO (FM)

WAJC / 104.5mc
502 W. 49th St.
Indianapolis, IN 46208
283-9292

Joseph Farah
Student operated

WFBQ (Q-95) / 94.7mc
6161 Fall Creek Road
Indianapolis, IN 46220
257-7565

Scott Hamilton (see WNDE)
95 seconds
Aud. 18-34; consumer-oriented

WFMS / 95.5mc
8120 Knue Road
Indianapolis, IN 46250
842-9550

Peter Miles
30 MINUTES WITH . . .

WICR / 88.7mc
1400 E. Hanna Avenue
Indianapolis, IN 46227
788-3280

Steve Campbell
STAR SPANGLED BANNER, current events show

WNAP / 93.1mc
9292 N. Meridian St.
Indianapolis, IN 46260
844-7200

John Osler
SPOTLIGHT INDIANAPOLIS
(w/Jaycees—see WIBC)

WNON / 101.9mc
P.O. Box 277
Indianapolis, IN 46052
873-2590

David DePoy
COFFEE WITH BARB (Barbara Smith)

WTLC / 105.7mc　　　　　Al Hobbs
P.O. Box 697　　　　　　LIKE IT IS (Gene Slaymaker)
Indianapolis, IN 46206
924–1456

WXIR　　　　　　　　　David White
4802 W. 62nd St.　　　　Christian format (see WBRI)
Indianapolis, IN 46220
255–5484

WXTZ / 103mc　　　　　Tom Severino
4560 Knollton Road　　　WEEKEND REPORT
Indianapolis, IN 46208
927–4200

WIAN / 90.1mc　　　　　Donna Holdych
931 Fletcher Avenue　　　INDIANAPOLIS JOURNAL
Indianapolis, IN 46203
266–4141

WGAQ / 95.9mc　　　　　Tony Brown
P.O. Box 190　　　　　　DISTAFF SIDE (daily features for
Franklin, IN 46131　　　　women)
736–4040

WJEL / 89.1mc　　　　　Jay Arlan
1901 E. 86th St.　　　　　Washington Township schools
Indianapolis, IN 46240
259–5278

WENS　　　　　　　　　Gene Olson
2255 N. Hawthorne Ln.
Indianapolis, IN 46218

WZPL　　　　　　　　　David Hutchinson
1440 N. Meridian St.
Indianapolis, IN 46202

RADIO (AM)

WATI / 810kc　　　　　Bob Todd, program director
3490 Bluff Road　　　　INDY INQUIRY, public affairs
Indianapolis, IN 46217　(Roger Coleman, host)
783–9284

WBRI / 1500kc
4802 E. 62nd St.
Indianapolis, IN 46220
255-5485

Gary Sallee
Christian format

WIBC / 1070kc
9292 N. Meridian St.
Indianapolis, IN 46260
844-7200

Jack Morrow, program oper. mgr.
FIRST DAY
SPOTLIGHT INDIANAPOLIS
(w/Jaycees)

WFMB / 1110kc
830 Logan St.
Noblesville, IN 46060
773-7444

Michael J. Mathis
CAROLYN CHURCHMAN SHOW

WMLF / 1310kc
1440 N. Meridian St.
Indianapolis, IN 46202
637-1375

WIRE / 1430kc
4650 Knollton Road
Indianapolis, IN 46208
927-4200

Bob Wise, public service
SUNDAY INDIANAPOLIS

WNDE / 1260kc
6161 Fall Creek Road
Indianapolis, IN 46220

Scott Hamilton
CONTACT
INSIDE INDIANAPOLIS
PERSPECTIVE INDIANAPOLIS

WNTS / 1590kc
4800 E. Raymond St.
Indianapolis, IN 46203
359-5593

Morgan Frye
Christian format

WXLW / 950kc
3003 Kessler Blvd., N.
Indianapolis, IN 46222
925-6494

Ed Sears, general mgr.
Gospel format

HANDOUTS will be used at both events. Quantity needed: 500.

A CASE STUDY

EVALUATION: Set historical with number in attendance, response rate to direct mail, gross income, and net income. Spiritual: Trust the Lord to provide case studies of positive effects of the events.

BUDGET: Donor to contribute printing costs; office funds to cover additional expenses.

CREATIVE:

ANNOUNCEMENTS AT CHURCH will be made impromptu.

BULLETIN ANNOUNCEMENTS

> Headline: Christian educator to speak on moral development of children
>
> Copy: Are you concerned with the moral development of your children? One of the nation's leading Christian educators will present a seminar on this important subject here at the Crossing Thursday, Feb. 21 at 7:30 p.m. For more information, contact Jan Cox.

CHURCH NEWSLETTER: Feb. 1: Pick up copy from bulletin; add paragraph on professional seminar:

> Are you concerned with the moral development of your children? One of the nation's leading Christian educators will present a seminar on this important subject here at the Crossing Thursday, Feb. 21 at 7:30 p.m.
>
> Dr. Ted Ward of Michigan State University will also present a half-day workshop for education professionals the following morning at 9 a.m. to noon.
>
> The Thursday Parent Enrichment Program is free and everyone is welcome. The professional workshop costs $10 and requires preregistration.

For more information, contact Jan Cox or call the church office at 844–9355.

Feb. 15 issue: Use same story that we'll submit as a feature to local publications.

Author, Lecturer

Expert on Moral Development of Children to Speak

By JIM VITTI

He has spent over 30 years studying the family, has directed a Lilly Endowment Study on values development, and has participated in two White House Conferences on the Family. Yet he claims the most profound counsel he'd give to any parent can be summed up in a simple, three-letter word.

"If I could give one specific piece of advice to parents, it would be to ask, 'Why?'" said Dr. Ted Ward, a professor of education at Michigan State University and

-more-

A CASE STUDY

WARD — add 1

an internationally acclaimed author, speaker, and authority on moral values development and nonformal education.

"The major role a parent can play with children is sharing of reasoning," Ward said. "There is no more important question than 'Why?' 'Why do you do that? Why do you think she wants that?'

"Sometimes parents grow tired of the child constantly asking 'Why?' but the parents should ask 'Why?' too. Parents should <u>not</u> think their major role is correcting, but to let the child <u>see</u> the consequences. If a child does not challenge reasoning, the child won't develop a mature values structure.

"A childish notion is able to produce moral behavior out of habit without moral reasoning behind it," he said.

Ward will be in Indianapolis this month to share his

-more-

WARD—add 2

insights with parents and health/education professionals. He'll be making two presentations: the first, a parent enrichment program on "The Impact of the Home on the Moral Development of Children," will be held Thursday evening, February 21, from 7 to 9 p.m. at the Church at the Crossing on the northeast side.

Ward's second talk, a workshop for professionals such as educators, counselors, and clerics, will be the following morning from 9 a.m. to noon at the same location. Dr. Phillip J. McDaniel, Washington Township superintendent, will give the welcome.

The professional workshop is entitled "Moral and Ethical Development: The Role of the Professional in Enabling Persons Growing Toward Wholeness."

A father of five and a grandfather of five more, Ward has firsthand experience, too. "But I'm not sure we learn

-more-

WARD — add 3

to be better parents by experience," he said. "In raising the fifth child, I wouldn't say we were more competent than with the first."

Ward said he would "try more carefully to keep in touch with their reasoning as they grew up" if he had an opportunity to start over as a parent, but there's only so much parents can expect of themselves.

"If I had it to do over again, I'd probably make different mistakes," he laughed.

But Ward does caution parents about feeling guilty.

"I doubt there's a parent alive who doesn't have that feeling from time to time," he said. "I don't say that critically, but sympathetically. It is destructive to be too self-critical because of what you did or didn't do as a parent.

"You have influence, but you can't control. We all

-more-

WARD — add 4

have autonomous responsibility—so I don't have to stand judgment for what my children do."

That doesn't give parents a blanket excuse for irresponsibility, though. "If I neglected or injured them, that's different," Ward said. "But once you've accepted that they must be responsible for their own decisions, life can be more livable."

Ward does feel parents can take some positive steps to increase their children's chances of being happy, well-adjusted, successful individuals.

"The parents' role in the moral development of children," he said, "depends on the <u>consistency</u> of what sorts of behavior they encourage and discourage."

Children go through two major stages of moral development, Ward said, adding that parents will be better able to deal with specific situations "if they know

-more-

WARD — add 5

the ways children make moral decisions, and see how the child is reasoning about moral questions."

The first stage is "all children begin making moral choices in terms of self-interest—reward or avoidance of punishment. Unfortunately, some people never grow out of it, but continue that through life. That is a retarded moral development, and a substantial number of adults suffer that problem."

The second level, Ward said, usually begins to develop between the ages of six and 16.

"It's more socially oriented," he said, "meaning it's based on how others look at us and our actions. That's why children in late childhood and early adolescence are so intensely attuned to their peers and models provided by others."

Ward sees positive value to peer pressure—even

-more-

WARD — add 6

negative influences. "We hope our children aren't getting too much bad exposure," he said, "but if children are only around a certain type, they don't get exposed to the challenging they need to develop. They need some bad influences."

Ward related this philosophy to physical development. "You don't get stronger by standing still, but by exercise," he said. "The parallel in the ethical realm says people need to make mistakes. Where there is no freedom to make mistakes, there is no freedom to grow."

There is one influence Ward believes children should be exposed to a great deal less.

"TV produces a very passive, observer class," he said, noting he's seen a change in his students over the last several years. "Today's generation has to be entertained and has a reduced capacity to do and create."

-more-

WARD — add 7

After nearly 30 years teaching at Michigan State, Ward has accepted a position at Trinity Evangelical Divinity School in Deerfield, Illinois. At the end of a two-year transition period, he'll take over as Dean of International Studies and Programs.

A devout Christian, Ward also serves as Chairman of the National Task Force of Evangelicals on the Family—and he considers moral development and Scripture inseparable.

"There are five empirical aspects of human growth—aspects we can measure, or put a finger on," he said. "These are physical, mental, emotional, social, and moral.

"The integrator that holds all these together is the spiritual part of us. You don't deal with the spiritual directly, but indirectly—by way of the five 'fingers.'"

-more-

WARD — add 8

Ward said none of the five aspects of growth is significantly more important than any of the others; all must receive equal emphasis. "There is a hazard of dealing with the whole person via just one or two of the 'fingers,'" he said. "We must use all of them."

Ward's emphasis on developing the spiritual aspect of people comes from the Bible. "In my book <u>Values Begin at Home,</u> there's an entire chapter devoted to the Ten Commandments," he said, "not as restrictions, but as liberating.

"If we look at them as good advice, that frees us to live life more fully and more thoroughly," he said. "It's a master guidebook to the reality of the human experience.

"Life without biblical guidance is like the father on Christmas morning who hasn't assembled the toy under the tree. He scrounges through the box and can't find a

-more-

A CASE STUDY

WARD — add 9

piece or two—life's like that—a bunch of pieces on the floor. Biblical truth is like finding that marvelous, valuable instruction sheet that says how to do it."

Ward's talks will be given at 9111 North Haverstick. For more information, call 844-9355.

-30-

DIRECT MAIL

Two different packages will be sent: one to church members (version A), one to professionals (version B). Each will consist of outer envelope, brochure, reply device, and cover letter. The same outer envelope and brochure will be used for both; cover letter and reply device will vary.

OUTER ENVELOPE: Use church stationery.

BROCHURE: Use illustration of classroom, looking over child's shoulder at teacher; child has photo of family on desk, as adult would (see illustration).

REPLY DEVICE for the parent program (church mailing): A facsimile "ticket" for admission (see illustration).

REPLY DEVICE for professional mailing: A reply envelope and registration card.

POSTERS will be same as the mailed brochure.

PRESS RELEASE and PSAs (see examples).

HANDOUTS at both events will be one color (black) due to costs and anticipated turnouts (see illustration).

Brochure

A CASE STUDY

Reply Device for Parents

Envelope Copy

```
                                              PLACE
                                              STAMP
                                              HERE

            The Church at the Crossing
            9111 N. Haverstick
            Indianapolis, IN 46240

            Attn: Professional workshop
```

Card Copy

What are your children learning at home?

The impact of the home on the moral development of children is overlooked more and more often these days. Find out what one expert learned in a Lilly endowment study and years of professional experience.

Please check the appropriate box or boxes.

☐ I'd like to attend the Parent Enrichment program **Thursday, Feb. 21, from 7 p.m. to 9 p.m.** I plan to attend along with ____ other guests.

☐ I'd like to attend the Professional Workshop **Friday, Feb. 22, from 9 a.m. to noon.** Enclosed is a $10 check (payable to The Early Childhood Center) so I'll be pre-registered.

☐ I'd like to know more about The Early Childhood Center and/or The Family Life Center. Please contact me.

Name_____
Address_____
City_____ State_____ Zip_____
Phone #_____

Please return in the enclosed self-addressed envelope by Friday, Feb. 15.

PUBLICITY HANDBOOK FOR CHURCHES

Letter to Parents

January 28, 1985

Dear Parent:

Have you ever wondered how much impact you and your home life are having on the moral development of your children?

If so, here's some exciting news. A leading educator and researcher will be in Indianapolis soon to provide some solutions to practical parenting needs.

His name is Dr. Ted Ward, and he's a Michigan State University professor, two-time White House Conference on the Family participant, and Lilly Endowment scholar.

Dr. Ward's presentation "Impact of the Home on the Moral Development of Children," will be held on Thursday evening, February 21, from 7:00 P.M. -9:00 P.M. at The Church at the Crossing, 9111 N. Haverstick, Indianapolis.

Admission is free, and a ticket good for your whole family is enclosed. Of course, a $5.00 donation per family will be appreciated to offset expenses.

In addition, Dr. Ward will lead a professional workshop the following morning from 9:00 A.M. to noon. Dr. Phillip J. McDaniel, Superintendent of the Metropolitan School District of Washington Township will be on hand to give the welcome.

I'd like to encourage you to come to the Parent Enrichment Program on Thursday, February 21. It's sure to be a valuable time for anyone interested in being an effective parent.

Sincerely,

Jan Cox, M.S., Director
Early Childhood Center

Juanita Leonard, A.C.S.W., Director
Family Life Center

P.S. BE SURE TO MARK YOUR CALENDAR FOR THURSDAY EVENING, FEBRUARY 21 FOR THE INFORMATIVE PARENT ENRICHMENT PROGRAM.

9111 N. Haverstick • Indianapolis, IN 46240 • 317/844-9355
Dr. G. David Cox, Senior Pastor • Rev. James R. Martin, Worship and Administration Ministries
Rev. Maxine G. Jones, Christian Education and Support Group Ministries • Rev. Kurt A. Salierno, Youth and Evangelism Ministries
Rev. Lori E. Salierno, Youth and Single Young Adult Ministries • Rev. Juanita L. Leonard, Missions Ministries

A CASE STUDY

Letter to Professionals

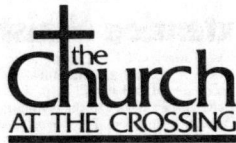

January 28, 1985

Dear Colleague:

One of the nation's leading experts on moral values development and non-formal education will lead a three-hour professional workshop in Indianapolis this month.

Dr. Ted Ward, A Lilly endowment scholar at Michigan State University, and two-time White House Conference on the family participant, will lead the workshop on "Moral and Ethical Development: The Role of the Professional in Enabling Persons Growing Toward Wholeness".

Dr. Phillip J. McDaniel, Superintendent of the Metropolitan School District of Washington Township will be the keynote speaker.

The program will take place on Friday, February 22, from 9:00 A.M. to noon, at the Church at the Crossing, 9111 N. Haverstick, Indianapolis. Registration is $10 per person and is tax-deductible as a business-related expense.

To guarantee a reservation, please return the enclosed pre-registration form immediately. We've enclosed a self-addressed envelope for your convenience. Please return the form by Friday, February 15, so we can plan appropriately.

In addition, Dr. Ward will give a brief "Parent Enrichment" talk the preceding evening, Thursday, February 21, 7:00 - 9:00 P.M. It's on "Impact of the Home on the Moral Development of Children". Of course, you're welcome to attend this event, as well.

I look forward to seeing you at the professional workshop, Friday morning, February 22.

Sincerely,

Jan Cox, M.S., Director
Early Childhood Center

Juanita Leonard, A.C.S.W., Director
Family Life Center

P.S. We're anticipating a large turnout with substantial media coverage for the professional workshop, so be sure to pre-register so you'll be able to join Dr. Ward and Dr. McDaniel.

Handout

Why Extension Ministry?

The Extension Ministries of The Church at the Crossing are an outgrowth of ministry to the larger community.

These ministries are led and staffed by professionally trained persons who offer to the church family and to the community professional services with Biblical, Christian orientation. The extension ministries are supported by fees generated by their services. The space and utilities are provided by the church.

I am delighted by the quality of services that we are able to offer to you through these extension ministries. They are designed to meet your family needs and to provide enrichment and quality of life for you.

I encourage you to explore the possibilities for your family.

Sincerely,

Senior Pastor
The Church at the Crossing

The Early Childhood Center.
In the early years, the child becomes a person whom he himself recognizes as separate from every other person. During this process the child has been growing in curiosity, in confidence, in caring. Responses to the child have helped to form an image of who he or she is, and the child, hopefully, sees a positive picture.

Adults who relate on a continuing basis to young children have the opportunity and responsibility to help a child build a healthy self — health that can serve for a lifetime. And that's our goal at the Church at the Crossing Early Childhood Center.

Opportunities for families at the Early Childhood Center include Mothers' Day Out; Preschool classes for 3-4 year olds; Parent and professional enrichment programs; Outdoor education, including an 18-acre facility and plans for a 10,000 square foot playscape.

The Family Life Center.
Christ came that we might have life and have it more abundantly.

At The Church at the Crossing Family Life Center, we share that vision. The center exists primarily to enable individuals, married couples and families to find greater meaning and fulfillment in life through discovering and developing the potential for growth which all persons have within themselves.

To accomplish these goals, we offer individual, marital and family therapy; personal growth groups; marital and family enrichment experiences; and workshops, conferences and short courses.

For more information, call, write, or stop by. The Church at The Crossing, 9111 North Haverstick, Indianapolis, IN 46240. (317) 844-9355.

A CASE STUDY

FOR IMMEDIATE RELEASE

CONTACT: Jan Cox,

Early Childhood Center,

844-9355

LILLY ENDOWMENT SCHOLAR/WHITE HOUSE
CONFEREE TO SPEAK ON MORAL DEVELOPMENT

INDIANAPOLIS—A Lilly Endowment scholar and two-time White House Conference on the family participant will report his findings on the moral development of children in Indianapolis this month.

Dr. Ted Ward, a Michigan State professor who has written and lectured extensively on moral values development and nonformal education, will speak twice—once to parents and once to professionals—on February 21 and 22.

Ward's first talk, geared toward parents, is on "the impact of the home on the moral development of children." His main focus will be his contention that simply

-more-

WARD — add 1

by asking their children "Why?" parents can help shape proper value structures.

The next day, Ward will lead a professional seminar on "moral and ethical development: the role of the professional in enabling persons toward wholeness." He will explain the empirical and nonempirical aspects of human growth and how educators, counselors, health professionals, and clerics can use those aspects to better understand and deal with children and families.

Dr. Philip J. McDaniel, Superintendent of Washington Township Schools, will deliver introductory remarks at the professional workshop.

Both events will take place at the Church at the Crossing, 9111 N. Haverstick on the northeast side. The parent program will be from 7 to 9 p.m. on Thursday, February 21.

-more-

WARD — add 2

The professional workshop will be held from 9 a.m. to noon, Friday, February 22. A $10 registration fee is required for this event.

For more information, contact Jan Cox at 844-9355.

-30-

PSA :10

Are you concerned with the moral development of children?

One of the nation's top experts on values development in the home will be speaking in Indianapolis February 21st and 22nd. For more information, call 844-9355.

###

PSA :30

Are you concerned with the moral development of children? One of the nation's top experts on values development in the home will be speaking in Indianapolis February 21st and 22nd.

His name is Dr. Ted Ward, and he's a Lilly Endowment scholar, noted author, and participant in the White House Conference on the Family.

His years of study will help you see ways to become a more effective parent or counselor.

To find out more information, call 844-9355. That's 844-9355. It's an event any parent won't want to miss.

###

A CASE STUDY

PRODUCTION SCHEDULE/BUDGET:

Fri.	12/21	Concept approved
Fri.	12/28	Photo shoot completed
Fri.	1/4	Copy finished; send to typesetter
Thurs.	1/10	Receive type; compose final art
Fri.	1/11	Four-color final art (brochure only) to printer
Thurs.	1/17	Receive chromalin (proof); proceed to production
Fri.	1/18	Complete final art for other materials; to printer
Fri.	1/25	Photocopy or mimeograph letters at church
Mon.	1/28	Stuff letters and mail
Fri.	2/15	"Deadline" for responses
Thurs.	2/21	Parent event
Fri.	2/22	Professional workshop
Mon.	2/25	Tally quantitative results

PRESS RELEASE: Mail late week of 2/4

PSA: Mail late week of 2/4

FOLLOW-UP: Phone calls for both, late week of 2/11

PRINTING COSTS: *(4-Color brochure)*

Color separations:	$550
Type:	100
Printing:	450
Total:	$1,100

EVALUATION:

Approximately 250 people attended the Parent Enrichment Program; donations totaled $1,090.

This attendance total cannot be specifically related to direct mail, since other media contributed heavily to attendance.

However, direct mail (with other media support) can be evaluated more specifically for the professional workshop.

Of 300 packages mailed, 77 people attended. This is a phenomenal 25.7 percent response rate and yielded $770 in gross income.

The total program brought in $1,870. Over 300 people attended the events. Comments and other reactions were all very positive.

The events were tremendous successes—the program worked!

APPENDIX 2

Fill-in Forms: A Guide

To make your first project easier, the next few pages include a general outline of how to put things together by filling in the blanks. If you find it helpful, you are free to use it over and over again. A copying machine that can enlarge material would be useful for making this matter closer to 8½" x 11" size.

STEPS TO A SUCCESSFUL PROMOTION

1. Prayer (list specifics)

   _____

   _____

   _____

2. The Marketing Plan

HISTORICAL INFORMATION

_____

_____

_____

_____

OBJECTIVES

Persuade _____ to _____

_____

STRATEGY

Media	Yes	No	Notes
ANNOUNCEMENTS AT CHURCH	___	___	___
CHURCH BULLETIN	___	___	___
CHURCH NEWSLETTER	___	___	___
DIRECT MAIL	___	___	___
POSTERS	___	___	___
PRESS RELEASES/NEWSPAPERS	___	___	___
PRESS RELEASES/MAGAZINES	___	___	___
PSAs/RADIO	___	___	___
PSAs/TV	___	___	___
HANDOUTS/FLYERS	___	___	___
OTHER MEDIA (specify)	___	___	___

TACTICS

ANNOUNCEMENTS AT CHURCH will be made on (dates) _____, _____, _____, and _____

THE CHURCH BULLETIN will mention the event on (dates) _____, _____, _____, and _____

THE CHURCH NEWSLETTER will mention the event in the _____ issue.

DIRECT MAIL will go to _____ church members, _____ members of the community, and _____ others.

POSTERS will be placed at _____

FILL-IN FORMS

PRESS RELEASES will be mailed to newspapers ―――――

—will be mailed to magazines ―――――――――

—follow-up phone calls will be made ――――――

PRESS RELEASES will be mailed to the following newspapers:

Newspaper/Address/Phone	Issue Date	Contact
_____	_____	_____
_____		
_____		
_____		
_____	_____	_____
_____		
_____		
_____		
_____	_____	_____
_____		
_____		
_____		
_____	_____	_____
_____		
_____		
_____		

PRESS RELEASES will be mailed to the following magazines and miscellaneous publications:

Publication/Address/Phone	Issue Date Deadline	Contact
_____	_____	_____
_____	_____	
_____		
_____		
_____	_____	_____
_____	_____	
_____		
_____		
_____	_____	_____
_____	_____	
_____		
_____		
_____	_____	_____
_____	_____	
_____		
_____		

PSAs will be mailed to the following radio stations:

Station/Address/Phone	Letters AM/FM	Contact Program

FILL-IN FORMS

_____

_____

_____ _____ _____

_____ _____ _____

_____

_____

_____ _____ _____

_____ _____ _____

_____

PSAs will be mailed to the following television stations:

Station/Address/Phone	**Channel**	**Contact Program**
_____	_____	_____
_____		_____
_____		
_____		
_____	_____	_____
_____		_____
_____		
_____		

FILL-IN FORMS

HANDOUTS/FLYERS will be distributed _____. Quantity will be _____.

OTHER MEDIA will be used as follows: _____
_____
_____

EVALUATION

Evaluation of event's success will be based on the following criteria: _____
_____
_____

BUDGET

Budget is limited to $_____ to cover _____
_____. Office funds available/not available to cover additional expenses such as postage, photocopies, and paper.

CREATIVE

ANNOUNCEMENTS AT CHURCH

COPY: _____
_____
_____
_____
_____
_____

BULLETIN ANNOUNCEMENTS

COPY: _____

_____

_____

_____

_____

_____

CHURCH NEWSLETTER

HEADLINE: _____

COPY: _____

_____

_____

_____

_____

_____

_____

FILL-IN FORMS

DIRECT MAIL

The mailing will comprise the following:

Component	Yes	No
Outer envelope	_____	_____
Brochure	_____	_____
Cover letter	_____	_____
Reply device	_____	_____
Publisher's note	_____	_____
Other element (specify)	_____	_____

OUTER ENVELOPE: Use church stationery/create new stationery. If new, specify: _____

COVER LETTER: Use church stationery/create new stationery. If new, specify: _____

BROCHURE

Major benefit: _____

Art: _____

_____

Headline: _____

Copy: _____

_____

_____

_____

_____

_____
_____
_____
_____
_____
_____
_____
_____
_____
_____
_____
_____

REPLY DEVICE will be constituted as follows:

Component	**Yes**	**No**
Reply envelope	_____	_____
Registration/order card	_____	_____
Reply card only	_____	_____
Other (specify)	_____	_____

Envelope copy:

_____
_____
_____
_____

FILL-IN FORMS

Card copy:

Headline: _____

Copy: _____

_____

_____

_____

_____

COVER LETTER will be 1 page / 2 pages / other (specify).

Cover letter copy:

Dear _____,

_____

_____

_____

_____

_____

_____

_____

_____

_____

_____

_____

P.S. _____

_____

POSTERS will/will not be the same as the mailed brochure. If not, specify.

Headline: _____

Copy: _____

_____

_____

_____

_____

_____

_____

_____

_____

FILL-IN FORMS

PRESS RELEASES

5W's: Who? _____

What? _____

Where? _____

When? _____

Why? _____

<u>FOR IMMEDIATE RELEASE</u>

CONTACT: _____

(___)_____

Headline: _____

Copy: _____

_____

_____

_____

_____

_____

_____

_____

_____

_____

_____

PSA: :30 copy

<u>FOR IMMEDIATE RELEASE</u>
CONTACT: _____
(_____)_____

Headline: _____

Copy: _____

_____

_____

_____

_____

_____

_____

_____

PSA: :10 copy

<u>FOR IMMEDIATE RELEASE</u>
CONTACT: _____
(_____)_____

Headline: _____

Copy: _____

_____

_____

_____

###

FILL-IN FORMS

HANDOUT/FLYER

Headline: _____

Copy: _____

_____

_____

_____

_____

_____

_____

_____

_____

_____

_____

_____

_____

OTHER MEDIA (specify)

Copy: _____

_____

_____

_____

PRODUCTION SCHEDULE/BUDGET

Date begun/ completed **Action**

_____ _____
_____ _____
_____ _____
_____ _____
_____ _____
_____ _____
_____ _____
_____ _____
_____ _____
_____ _____
_____ _____
_____ _____

PRESS RELEASE: Mail (date) _____

PSA: Mail (date) _____

Follow-up phone calls (date) _____

PRINTING COSTS:

Item   **Cost**

_____ _____
_____ _____
_____ _____

FILL-IN FORMS

_____ _____
_____ _____
_____ _____

                        TOTAL _____

EVALUATION

_____
_____
_____
_____
_____
_____
_____

APPENDIX 3

Glossary of Terms

ADVERTISING STYLE (ch. 5)—The style of writing that uses characteristics unique to presenting a motivating message.

BENEFITS (ch. 5)—Good things a product, service, or event can do for the target audience. Benefits motivate people to take action; features do not.

BLEED (ch. 8)—When a photograph or other form of artwork extends to and past the edge of a printed page.

BROADCAST STYLE (ch. 5)—The style of writing used for television and radio announcements.

BUDGET (ch. 3)—All funds available for advertising efforts, including general office materials.

CALL TO ACTION (ch. 5)—The element of copy that directs the target audience to do something specific; a crucial element that should always be included.

CAMERA-READY ART (ch. 8)—The finished piece from which the others (such as brochures) will be produced. Also called final art and pasteup.

CLASSIC FORMAT (ch. 7)—A traditionally effective direct-mail package, consisting of an outer envelope, cover letter, brochure, reply device, and sometimes publisher's note and/or involvement device.

COPY (ch. 5)—The words that made up an ad, press release, or PSA.

CROP (ch. 8)—To remove all unessential parts of a photograph.

DIRECT MAIL (ch. 4)—Any mass mailing (from postcards to elaborate packages) to promote an event, sell a product, or advertise a service.

GLOSSARY OF TERMS

EVALUATION (ch. 3)—The final part of a marketing plan; a comparison of the actual outcome against objectives.

FEATURES (ch. 5)—Descriptive items about a product, service, or event. Features must be turned into benefits to motivate a target audience.

FIVE W's (ch. 5)—In journalism style, "Who?" "What?" "When?" "Where?" and "Why?"; questions which must be answered within the first few paragraphs of a news story.

FORMAT (ch. 10)—Using several design elements that make more than one printed piece complement others.

FULFILLMENT (ch. 9)—Taking care of details after the advertising has taken place, such as keeping track of returned cards.

HALFTONE (ch. 6)—A photographic image of a picture made up of many tiny dots. It reproduces much better than a photo.

HISTORICAL INFORMATION (ch. 3)—The first part of a marketing plan, describing what has happened in the past to provide a good idea as to what works and what doesn't.

INVERTED PYRAMID (ch. 5)—Approach used in writing stories in journalism style, starting with general facts and getting more specific.

INVOLVEMENT DEVICE (ch. 4)—A piece included in a mailing that generates involvement on the part of the target audience, such as stickers and pull-tabs.

JOURNALISM STYLE (ch. 5)—The style of writing used for news stories. It involves the Five W's and the inverted pyramid.

LAYOUT (ch. 6)—Arrangement of all elements on a page or pages.

LEADING (ch. 8)—Spacing between lines of copy when typeset.

MARKETING PLAN (ch. 3)—A brief overview of how to promote an event; consists of historical information, objectives, strategy, tactics, evaluation, and budget.

MEDIA (ch. 4)—All the different ways to promote an event, such as newspapers, magazines, TV, radio, posters, direct mail, bulletins, announcements, newsletters, and other forms of communication. *Media* is the plural form of *medium*; each of the above list is a medium.

NESTLING (ch. 5)—Hiding short copy within long copy, such as using subheads to tell a complete story. It gets people who skim copy to see key points.

OBJECTIVES (ch. 3)—The main point of our activity, spelled out in a statement that is part of the marketing plan.

OFFSET (ch. 8)—Short for offset lithography, a common and relatively inexpensive method of printing.

OVERLAY (ch. 8)—Also called a color overlay; used with a layout when a second color will be used.

PASTEUP (ch. 8)—Another name for camera-ready art or final art.

POINTS (ch. 8)—A measurement used to distinguish sizes of type. There are 72 points to an inch.

PRESS RELEASE (ch. 4)—A news story sent to a newspaper or magazine editor, designed to get free advertising.

PRODUCTION SCHEDULE (ch. 8)—A timetable indicating when materials need to be completed at each stage of development.

PSA (ch. 4)—Public Service Announcement; a news story sent to a radio or TV station and designed to get "free advertising."

PUBLISHER'S NOTE (ch. 7)—A part of a direct-mail package, often using a testimonial, to further promote a product, service, or event.

REPLY DEVICE (ch. 7)—A part of a direct-mail package consisting of either a reply card or a reply form with reply envelope.

RUBDOWN LETTERING (ch. 6)—Alphabets for pressing down on paper that can be used easily and inexpensively to make headlines on camera-ready art.

SELF-MAILER (ch. 7)—A less expensive yet usually less effective direct-mail format, comprising one sheet of paper, folded over, used as both brochure and "envelope."

SERIFS (ch. 6)—Tiny "feet" on letters and numbers of some typefaces that make them easier to read than sans-serif ("without serif") typefaces.

SPEC (ch. 8)—Short for *specify*; we "spec" type as to typeface, size, and leading.

STRATEGY (ch. 4)—A part of the marketing plan that lists which media to use.

TACTICS (ch. 4)—A part of the marketing plan that specifies how and when each medium will be used.

TARGET AUDIENCE (ch. 3)—The people toward whom publicity and communication are directed.

GLOSSARY OF TERMS

TELEMARKETING (ch. 9)—Using the telephone to complement a marketing effort.

TYPE (ch. 6)—All the letters that make up copy.

TYPEFACE (ch. 8)—One of several hundred different-looking forms of type, complete with an alphabet and numbers.

TYPESETTING (ch. 6)—Putting copy into neat, even columns for camera-ready art.

WASTE (ch. 3)—People who hear a message but are not a part of the target audience.